D1342379

Surgical Vivas for ST Trainees

GOOD HOPE HOSPITAL LIBRARY

Shahab Khan

UMFUNDISI
PUBLICATIONS

First published in 2008
by Umfundisi Publications
8 Temple Square
Aylesbury
United Kingdom
HP20 2QH

British Library Cataloguing in Publication Data

A catalogue record for this book is available from the British Library.

ISBN 978-1-905235-03-2

Contents

4. Limb Anatomy

Part 2: Critical Care

Part 3: Physiology

Part 4: Pathology

Introduction

Times are changing in surgical training. The current hiatus with the new Modernising Medical Careers is causing a stir in the surgical world with uncertainty for all. There is currently very little in the way of formal information regarding the intricacies of the new training scheme for surgeons in the United Kingdom. The 'old' IMRCS is due to cease in 2010 with a new assessment scheme coming into place.

The Royal Colleges have issued some guidance as to the types of assessment that are likely to take place in the new scheme. It seems that the 'old' MRCS Part 1 and Part 2 are to be replaced by a similar examination which is intended to be taken by the end of ST1. The 'Viva' Exam is to be replaced by a similar oral examination that is designed to be taken and passed during the ST2 year. Beyond this there is less in the way of concrete plans for assessment, though it is certain that further formal assessment will occur at the latter stages of ST training.

Examinations have always been a subject of much anxiety and fear amongst surgical trainees. They are difficult and often have low pass rates against a good cadre of candidate. They are also frequently a barrier to career progression and therefore the pressure to pass becomes increasingly high.

This book is written with the intention to being a revision aid for candidates studying for the new viva examination to be taken at ST2 level. It is written by surgical trainees who have been through surgical examinations and helped candidates prepare for examinations. The authors have consulted the Royal Colleges in terms of the exam structure and the book has been laid out accordingly. The content is relevant to everyday surgical practice, and focuses on improving candidates' grounding of basic surgical sciences. The topics covered are those which are commonly covered in surgical examinations and are vital to understand in order to pass. There is also a definite focus of attention on anatomy, as this is the area in which most candidates are weakest and least confident.

This book would be of benefit as a quick reference for core basic topics. Medical students wishing to impress at their surgical finals would also benefit from the contents. It is intended that the topics are covered in a self-testing or colleague-testing manner, thus improving the readers ability to verbalise thought and reason.

There have always been candidates who are very successful in examinations and there is no reason why you cannot be one of them. The exam may be changing but there are common strategies that you can use to improve your chances of success.

These are some of the top tips that you should follow in the lead-up to the exam:

- 'If you fail to prepare, prepare to fail.' An age-old quote that stands to reason. However it is always amazing to see candidates merely weeks before their Viva with no revision plan and very little work behind them.
- You need to be positive and believe that you CAN do it.
- Make sure that you maintain a good work/life balance. There is no point in burning yourself out before you step into the exam room.
- Don't give up. However badly you feel the Viva is going, remain confident and composed. It is impossible to tell how well or badly you are doing, so don't try. Let the examiners decide once you have left the room. Remember that you are marked on your responses for ALL the questions, not just one.
- Look the part. It is essential that you make a good impression by dressing smartly, being well presented and personable. After all, the examiners will be asking in the back of their minds, 'would I want this person to work for me?'.
- Practice vivas with friends, colleagues and senior staff. This is the most useful experience that you will get. Put yourself under pressure and get used to talking in these situations. If you have not been in this position before you will find it very stressful indeed.

- Try to enjoy the experience. After all, you have done a lot of hard work to get there. Make sure that you go into the exam with a view to showing the examiners how good your knowledge is.
- Lastly, put things in perspective. Whilst it may seem that failure would result in the end of the world, it won't. In fact it will probably make you a more knowledgeable and confident surgeon in the future.

We hope that you enjoy reading this book. We are sure it will give you a flavour for the common topics. Hopefully it will assist your success.

Good Luck!

Kevin McMillan MRCS
Shahab Khan MRCS

Contributors

Mr Thangadorai Amalesh MS MRCS
Specialist Registrar in General Surgery
North East Thames Rotation

Mr Ashley Brown MD FRCS
Consultant Surgeon
Southend University Hospital, Essex

Dr Shaifali Jain MRCP FRCR
Consultant Radiologist
Southend University Hospital, Essex

Mr Simranjeev Johal BSc MRCS
Senior House Officer in General Surgery
Addenbrooke's Hospital, Cambridge

Dr Alexander Stone FRCA
Consultant in Intensive Care Medicine & Anaesthetics
Southend University Hospital, Essex

A special word of recognition to **Dr M Hollands** MBBS for her detailed illustrations which we hope help to bring the text to life.

Part 1

Anatomy

Chapter 1

Abdomen

1: Stomach

What are the anatomical regions of the stomach?

The stomach starts at the cardia, where it forms the gastro-oesophageal junction. The right border of the cardia continues straight down to form the lesser curvature. The left border joins the greater curvature forming a discrete notch called the incisura cardiacum. Following this are the dome-like fundus, and the body of the stomach. The start of the pyloric antrum is evident externally from another notch, this time on the lesser curvature called the incisura angularis, The junction of the pylorus and the duodenum is indicated on the surface of the stomach by a circular constriction, and is also marked by an overlying constant vein (of Mayo).

What is the blood supply to the stomach?

The stomach is a derivative of the foregut and, therefore, derives its blood supply from the coeliac axis.

The left and right gastric arteries supply the lesser curvature.

The left and right gastroepiploic arteries supply the greater curvature.

The short gastric arteries supply the fundus of the stomach.

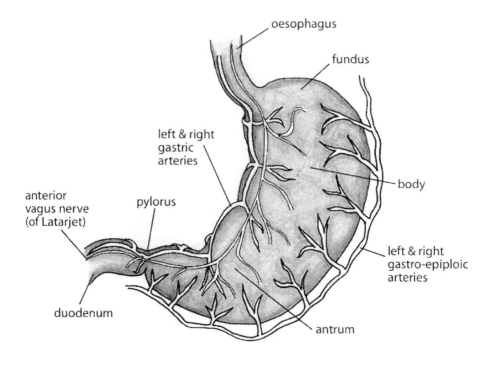

Figure 1: Anatomy of the stomach

Which secreting cell types can be found within the stomach?

Parietal cells – found at the fundus and body, secrete HCl and intrinsic factor.

G cells – found at the pylorus, secrete gastrin.

Chief cells – found at the fundus and body, secrete pepsinogen.

Mucus cells – secrete an alkaline mucus which protects against acidity in the stomach.

2: Pancreas

What are the anatomical regions of the pancreas, and describe its position in the abdomen?

The pancreas is a retroperitoneal organ lying on the transpyloric plane of Addison. It consists of a head and uncus (found at the level of L2), and a body and tail (found at L1 and L2).

Briefly describe the embryology of the pancreas?

The pancreas is a derivative of the foregut, which begins development during the 5th week of life. It forms from two buds of the endoderm, a larger dorsal diverticulum and smaller ventral diverticulum. Rotation of the ventral part occurs, allowing it to lie next to and inferior to the dorsal part. The two then fuse at around the 7th week of life, with communication of the ducts of Wirsung and Santorini.

What is the blood supply to the pancreas?

As mentioned, the pancreas is primarily a foregut structure but part of its head is derived from an outgrowth of the common bile duct. Its blood supply reflects this by being supplied from the coeliac axis as well as from the superior mesenteric artery.

Head – anastomosis between the superior pancreatoduodenal artery (coeliac axis) and the inferior pancreatoduodenal artery (superior mesenteric artery).

Body and Tail – from arteria pancreatica magna, which arises from the splenic artery.

Where does the portal vein form in relation to the pancreas?

The portal vein is formed by the splenic vein and the superior mesenteric vein, behind the neck of the pancreas. From here it travels to the liver via the porta hepatis (gateway to the liver).

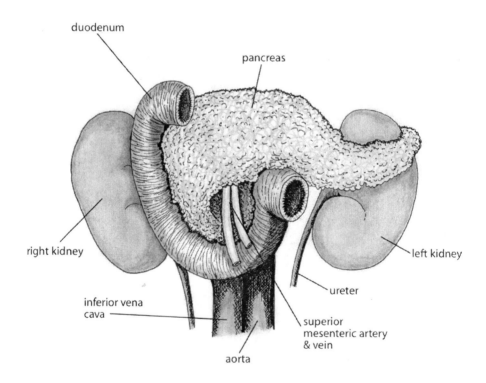

Figure 2: Anatomy of the pancreas

3: Spleen

How large is the spleen, and where in the abdomen is it found?

The spleen is found in the left hypochondrium. It measures 3×7×12 centimeters in size, but more conveniently remembered as 1×3×5 inches. It weighs roughly 5-7 ounces and is located behind the left 9th-11th ribs.

When palpating the spleen, what features help to identify it?

A spleen generally needs to be at least twice its normal size in order to be palpable. When enlarged, it can be felt as a smooth, firm swelling that arises from the left costal margin. It should descend with inspiration and a splenic notch can sometimes be felt. The examiner should not be able to get above the spleen.

What is the blood supply to the spleen?

For the purpose of blood supply, the spleen can be thought of as a foregut structure, although strictly speaking it is derived from the dorsal mesogastrium.

Its blood supply is derived from the splenic artery (tortuous branch of the coeliac axis), which divides into numerous smaller branches at the splenic hilum.

What are the causes of splenomegaly?

Splenomegaly can be divided into massive (classically >1000g) or mild/moderate (over 400g).

Causes of massive splenomegaly include:

- Malaria
- Visceral leishmaniasis (Kala Azar)
- Leukemia (CLL, CML)
- Lymphoma
- Myelofibrosis
- Polycythemia rubra vera

Causes of mild/moderate splenomegaly include:

- Vascular – hepatic/portal/splenic vein thrombosis
- Increased cell turnover – haemaglobinopathies
- Immune response – AIDS, tuberculosis, endocarditis
- Autoimmune – systemic lupus erythematosus, rheumatoid arthritis
- Metabolic disease – amyloidosis, Gaucher's disease

4: Blood supply to bowel

Briefly describe the blood supply of the GI tract?

The blood supply to the alimentary tract is defined by its embryological descent.

Foregut - Oesophagus to duodenum (entrance of common bile duct), supplied by coeliac axis

Midgut - Duodenum to transverse colon (two-thirds of the way along), supplied by superior mesenteric artery

Hindgut - Transverse colon to the upper rectum, supplied by inferior mesenteric artery

Describe the blood supply to the small bowel?

The duodenum gains its blood supply from the superior and inferior pancreatoduodenal arteries (being both foregut and midgut in origin).

The rest of the small bowel gains its blood supply from the jejunal and ileal branches of the superior mesenteric artery.

Describe the blood supply to the large bowel?

Similarly, the colon traverses the boundary between midgut and hindgut. The superior mesenteric artery gives off the ileocolic, the right colic and the middle colic arteries up to the transverse colon. The inferior mesenteric artery gives off the left colic artery which supplies the descending colon, and the sigmoidal artery which supplies the sigmoid colon.

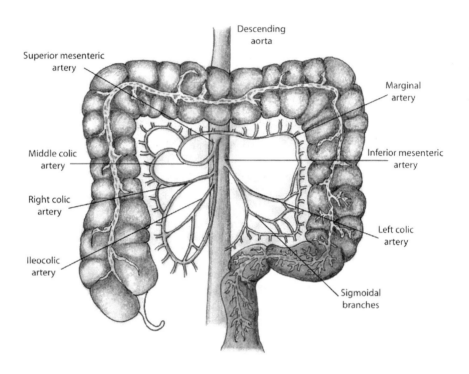

Figure 3: Blood supply to large intestines

What anastomosis occurs between the Superior Mesenteric Artery and Inferior Mesenteric Artery?

The anastomosis between the two is the marginal artery of Drummond, which occurs on the inner bowel along the entire colon. This is particularly weak at the splenic flexure and may even be non-existent.

Occasionally there is a secondary arterial cascade, initially called the arc of Riolan, but now more commonly referred to as the meandering mesenteric artery.

Describe the blood supply to the rectum?

The upper half of the rectum derives its blood supply from the superior rectal arteries (from the inferior mesenteric artery).

The lower half of the rectum derives its blood supply from the inferior and middle rectal arteries (from the internal iliac arteries).

The venous drainage follows the arterial pattern, and is thus a site of porto-systemic anastomosis.

5: Inguinal Region

Describe the boundaries of the inguinal canal.

The inguinal canal is a slit-like structure running obliquely between the deep and superficial rings.

Its boundaries are:

- *Anterior* – external oblique aponeurosis
- *Posterior* – conjoint tendon and transversalis fascia
- *Roof* – internal oblique and transversus muscle.
- *Floor* – Inguinal ligament

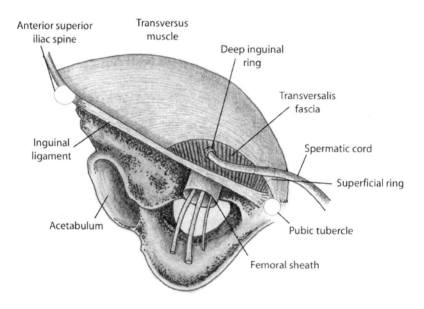

Figure 4: Anatomy of inguinal region
(internal and external oblique removed)

What are the surface markings of the deep and superficial inguinal rings?

Deep ring – a defect in the transversalis fascia found 1.25 cm above the mid-point of the inguinal ligament

Superficial ring – triangular opening in the external oblique located 1.0 cm above and lateral to the pubic tubercle.

What are the contents of the canal in the male?

Spermatic cord, which contains the following:

Vas deferens

Pampiniform plexus of veins

Lymphatics

Three arteries
- Testicular artery
- Artery to the vas
- Cremasteric artery

Three nerves
- Genital branch of genitofemoral nerve
- Sympathetics accompanying arteries
- Ilioinguinal nerve (strictly speaking this actually runs on and not in the spermatic cord)

6: Embryology of Gastro-Intestinal Tract

What are the boundaries of the foregut, midgut and hindgut?

Foregut – From the mouth to the 2nd part of duodenum (entrance of common bile duct)

Midgut – From the 2nd part of the duodenum to 2/3 along the transverse colon

Hindgut – From 2/3 along the transverse colon to the ectodermal part of anal canal

What phenomenon occurs in the alimentary tract during the 6th week of development?

During the 6th week, a physiological umbilical herniation occurs. As the gut rapidly elongates and the liver grows during this period, the contents are no longer able to remain inside the relatively small abdominal cavity. As a result a portion of the midgut herniates through into the umbilical cord.

After herniation, how is the midgut still attached to the abdomen and what is its clinical relevance?

This segment remains attached to the abdomen (specifically the yolk sac) via the vitello-intestinal duct. This will ordinarily degenerate during development. However, when this persists it remains as a Meckel's diverticulum.

Between the 10th and 12th weeks, the abdominal cavity is large enough to accommodate the bowel and the herniation spontaneously resolves. Upon returning, the midgut undergoes a 270° anticlockwise turn so that the proximal part goes to the bottom right and the distal segment goes to the top right.

7: Duodenum

What is the total length of the duodenum?

Total length of the duodenum is 25 cm, but it is more conveniently remembered in inches.

The word Duodenum derives from the Latin, Duodeni, meaning "twelve each" (initially estimated as being 12 finger-breadths long).

The duodenum is divided into four parts:
- D1 – 2 inches
- D2 – 3 inches
- D3 – 4 inches
- D4 – 1 inches

Where does the ampulla of Vater open?

It opens into the second part of the duodenum, roughly 10 cm from the pylorus.

What is the blood supply to the duodenum?

As the boundary between the foregut and the midgut is at the ampulla of Vater, the duodenum is therefore derived from both the foregut and the midgut.

Its blood supply reflects this:

1st part – gastroduodenal artery (foregut origin)

2nd, 3rd and 4th parts – superior and inferior pancreatoduodenal arteries (midgut origin)

What is the suspensory ligament of Treitz?

It is a band of connective muscular tissue from the right crus of the diaphragm attaching to the muscular coat of the duodeno-jejeunal flexure. When it contracts, it opens the DJ flexure, allowing passage of chyme.

8: The Biliary System and Lesser Sac

Describe the flow of bile from the liver to the duodenum?

Bile is produced by the liver at a rate of at least 500 mls per day. It exits via the left and right hepatic ducts, which join to form the common hepatic duct. From here the bile may flow into the gallbladder via the cystic duct where it can be stored. When it is needed, the gallbladder contracts, allowing bile to pass into the cystic duct and then into the common bile duct (a continuation of the hepatic duct beyond the entrance of the cystic duct). From here it passes through the ampulla of Vater into the posterolateral wall of the 2nd part of the duodenum.

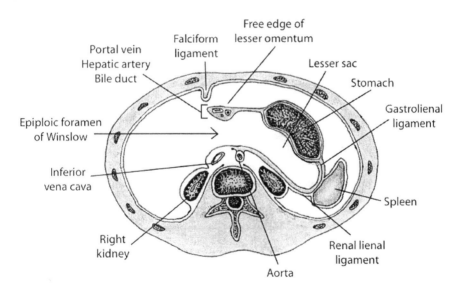

Figure 5: Cross-section of abdomen showing epiploic foramen and lesser sac

How does the bile duct pass in the lesser omentum?

The upper part of the bile duct passes within the free edge of lesser omentum along with the hepatic artery and the portal vein. This omentum and its contents form the anterior border of the epiploic foramen of Winslow.

The order in which they travel is
- Common bile duct – anteriorly and laterally
- Hepatic artery – anteriorly and medially
- Portal vein – posterior to the two

As well as being the most surgically accessible part of the bile duct, it is also the site at which the vessels can be easily located and compressed. This exercise is employed to reduce bleeding from the liver (Pringle's manoeuvre).

What is Calot's triangle?

This useful landmark is used in cholecystectomy in order to help delineate and locate anatomical structures, in particular, the cystic artery.

It is made up of: (a) Inferior edge of the liver
                      (b) Common hepatic duct
                      (c) Cystic duct

What are the boundaries of the foramen of Winslow?

The foramen of Winslow is a communication between the greater and lesser sacs of the abdomen. Its borders are:
- *Anterior:* free edge of lesser omentum
- *Posterior:* inferior vena cava
- *Superior:* caudate lobe of the liver
- *Inferior:* 1st part of duodenum

9: Urinary System

Describe the course of the ureters?

The ureter is approximately 25cm long.

After leaving the renal pelvis it descends along psoas major into the pelvis at the level of the common iliac bifurcation.

From here it passes along the outer wall of the pelvis toward the ischial spines.

It then passes medially to enter the fundus of the bladder.

What are the narrowest points of the ureter?

There are 3 main points where the ureter narrows. These are:

- Pelvi-ureteric junction
- Crossing of the pelvic brim
- Vesico-ureteric junction

Clinically this is important as renal calculi are more likely to impact at these sites.

What are the parts of the urinary bladder?

The bladder is an inverted pyramidal shape. It is composed of an apex, a base, a neck and a trigone.

What is the nerve supply to the bladder?

- *Motor* – parasympathetic via S2-S4 and sympathetic via L1-2
- *Sensory* – mainly from parasympathetic fibers with a small contribution from sympathetic

10: The Aorta

What are the branches of the thoracic aorta?

- Left and right coronary arteries
- Brachiocephalic trunk
- Left common carotid artery
- Left subclavian artery
- 3 paired arteries – bronchial, oesophageal and posterior intercostals arteries

What are the branches of the abdominal aorta?

- 3 single vessels: coeliac axis, superior mesenteric and inferior mesenteric arteries.
- 3 paired visceral branches: adrenal, renal and gonadal arteries.
- 5 paired abdominal wall branches: inferior phrenic and 4 lumbar arteries.
- Terminal branches: common iliac artery, median sacral artery.

At what levels do these vessels leave the abdominal aorta?

This can be conveniently remembered as the aorta tends to give off a branch at each level:

- T12 – passes through the diaphragmatic hiatus
      – gives off the coeliac axis
- L1 – gives off the superior mesenteric artery
- L2 – gives off the renal & gonadal arteries
- L3 – gives off the inferior mesenteric artery
- L4 – bifurcates into the common iliac arteries

11: CT abdomen

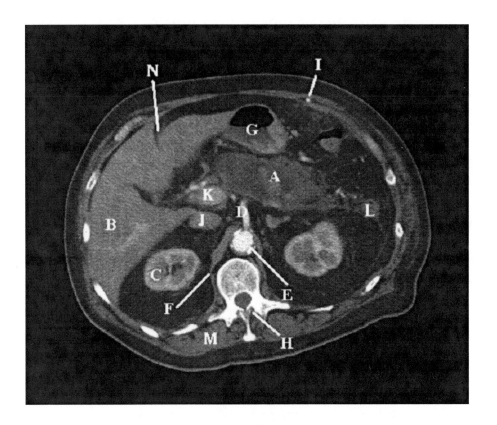

Figure 6: CT scan of the abdomen

Name the structures labeled on Figure 6?

A – pancreas
B – liver
C – right kidney
D – coeliac axis
E – abdominal aorta
F – left diaphragmatic crus
G – stomach

H – vertebra
I – superior epigastric artery
J – inferior vena cava
K – portal vein
L – descending colon
M – erector spinae muscles
N – falciform ligament

What pathology can be seen in the CT scan?

There is an acute grossly oedematous pancreas, with areas of patchy necrosis.

At what level of the abdomen is this CT slice?

It is approximately at the level of T12

Notable features at this level include
- Aorta passes through its diaphragmatic hiatus
- Coeliac axis leaves the aorta
- 12th rib attaches at T12 vertebra

Chapter 2

Thorax

1: Mediastinum

What are the compartments of the mediastinum?

The mediastinum is, in the first instance, divided into a superior and inferior mediastinum by an oblique line from the manubriosternal joint (angle of Louis) to the lower margin of the T4 vertebra.

The *inferior mediastinum* is further divided into anterior, middle and posterior compartments.

The *anterior mediastinum* is from the sternum to the pericardium.

The *middle mediastinum* is found between the two pericardial layers.

The *posterior mediastinum* is from the pericardium to the vertebra T5-T12

Briefly list the contents of each?

Superior mediastinum
Great vessels, oesophagus, trachea, phrenic and vagus nerves

Anterior mediastinum
Thymus, internal thoracic artery and lymph nodes

Middle mediastinum

Heart, ascending aorta, superior vena cava, pulmonary trunk, tracheal bifurcation and phrenic nerve

Posterior mediastinum

Descending aorta, oesophagus, azygous and hemiazygous veins, thoracic duct and vagus nerve

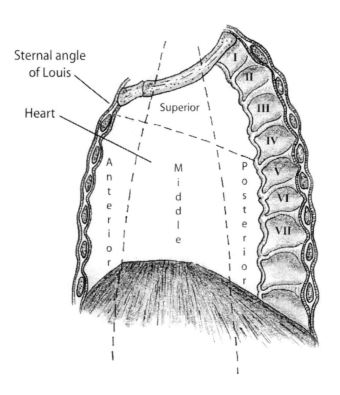

Figure 7: Compartments of the mediastinum

2: Lungs and Pleura

Describe the surface markings of the pleura?
How does this differ from that of the lungs?

On the right side, the pleura join at the following points:
- Behind the sternoclavicular joint down to the 2nd costal cartilage
- Vertically down to the 6th costal cartilage
- To the 8th rib in the mid-clavicular line
- To the 10th rib in the mid-axillary line
- To the 12th rib at the border of the erector spinae muscles

On the left, the path is similar except the heart must be accommodated. Therefore, the pleura travels from the 2nd to the 4th costal cartilages, but then deviates laterally and travels half way towards the apex of the heart.

Describe the anatomy of the lung root?
How do they differ on each side?

There are slight differences between the left and right lung roots arising from the fact that, on the right, the left upper bronchus (and artery) has already bifurcated.

**Right lung root
(from superior to inferior)**

(a) Right upper bronchus & pulmonary artery
(b) Right middle bronchus & pulmonary artery
(c) Pulmonary veins

**Left lung root
(from superior to inferior)**

(a) Pulmonary artery
(b) Left main bronchus
(c) Pulmonary vein

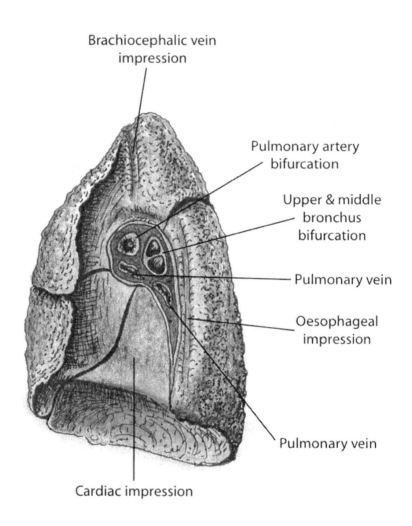

Figure 8: Hilum of right lung

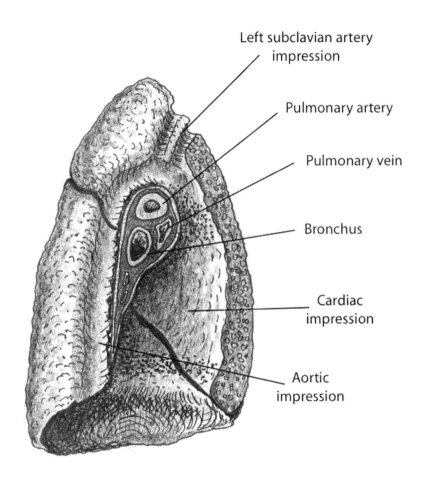

Figure 9: Hilum of left lung

3: Diaphragm

Briefly describe the embryology of the diaphragm?

The diaphragm arises from 4 main sources, starting at the 4th week and ending around the 7th week.

- Septum transversum – forming central tendon
- Pleuro-peritoneal membrane – covers pleuro-peritoneal canals
- Oesophageal mesentery – forms diaphragmatic crura
- Body wall – forms outer wall of diaphragm

What are the functions of the diaphragm?

- Inspiration/expiration – vital in the mechanics of breathing
- Abdominal effects – can be used to raise intra-abdominal pressure to aid vomiting, urination, parturition & defaecation
- Acts as a separating layer between abdomen and thorax
- Maintains the gastro-oesophageal angle

What is the nerve supply of the diaphragm?

Motor - from the phrenic nerve, mainly C4, with contributions from C3 and C5

Sensory - some proprioceptive fibers from intercostal (periphery) and phrenic (central) nerves

What is the blood supply of the diaphragm?

- Intercostal & subcostal arteries
- Inferior phrenic arteries
- Pericardiophrenic & musculophrenic arteries

What openings within the diaphragm are you aware of?

There are numerous openings within the diaphragm to allow passage of nerves and vessels.

These include

T8	T10	T12
Inferior vena cava	Oesophagus	Aorta
Right phrenic nerve	Left & right vagi	Thoracic duct
		Azygous vein

Several smaller openings are also present to allow passage of :

- Left phrenic nerve
- Hemiazygous vein
- Splanchnic nerve

4: Nerves in the Chest

What is the nerve root value of the phrenic nerve?

It originates from the 3rd, 4th and 5th cervical spinal nerves.

Describe the course of the phrenic nerve from its origin to the level of the diaphragm?

It is best to consider the left and right paths separately

RIGHT
(venous pathway)

(a) anterior to anterior scalenus muscle
(b) posterior to right brachiocephalic vein
(c) posterolateral to Superior vena cava
(d) lateral to right atrium
(e) lateral to inferior vena cava
(f) diaphragm

LEFT
(arterial pathway)

(a) anterior to anterior scalenus muscle
(b) anterior to left subclavian artery
(c) anterior to the aortic arch
(d) lateral to left ventricle
(e) diaphragm

What does the phrenic nerve supply in its course?

Motor – diaphragm

Sensory – diaphragm, pleura, pericardium and peritoneum

From where does the vagus nerve originate?

The vagus is the only cranial nerve to arise from the brainstem, emerging from the medulla oblongata. Interestingly, its name originates from the Latin meaning 'wandering' or 'vagrant' as it is thought to wander through the chest into the abdomen.

Describe the course of the vagus nerve from its origin to the level of the diaphragm?

Again, it is easier to describe the left & right separately.

RIGHT
- Through the jugular foramen
- Descends in the neck within the carotid sheath
- Gives off right recurrent laryngeal, which wraps around the right subclavian artery
- Descends para-tracheal
- Passes behind the lung
- Follows the oesophagus to pass through the diaphragm

LEFT
- Through the jugular foramen
- Descends in the neck within the carotid sheath
- Held away from the trachea by the subclavian and common carotid arteries
- At the aortic arch, left recurrent laryngeal nerve hooks around the ligamentum arteriosum
- Passes behind the lung
- Follows the oesophagus to pass through the diaphragm

What is the distal most point that the vagus supplies the bowel?

The vagus provides parasympathetic supply up to the splenic flexure of the large intestine. Thereafter, it is supplied by pelvic splanchnic nerves from the lateral horn of S2-4.

5: Heart

What are the surface markings of the boundaries of the heart?

This can be best described by mapping out 4 points in the chest, and connecting them with a line. These are:
- Right 3rd costal cartilage
- Right 6th costal cartilage
- Left 5th mid-clavicular line
- Left 2nd costal cartilage

What is the blood supply of the heart?

The blood supply is derived from the anterior and posterior aortic sinuses of Valsalva. The posterior sinus giving rise to the left coronary artery.

Left Coronary Artery (left main stem):
- Divides after approximately 2.0 cm in to the left anterior descending and circumflex arteries.
- The *left anterior descending artery* passes in interventricular groove. It anastomoses with posterior interventricular branch of the right coronary artery. It also gives off large diagonals during its course.
- The *circumflex* artery passes in the atrioventricular to anastomose with the right coronary artery. It gives off obtuse marginal branches.

Right Coronary Artery:
- Runs along the atrioventricular groove towards the inferior part of the heart
- Gives off the important sinoatrial node artery (60% of people)
- Gives off the posterior interventricular branch (usually)

The 'dominance' of the heart refers to which system gives off the posterior interventricular artery. This is usually the right coronary artery, but the circumflex artery provides this vessel in 10% of people, giving left heart dominance.

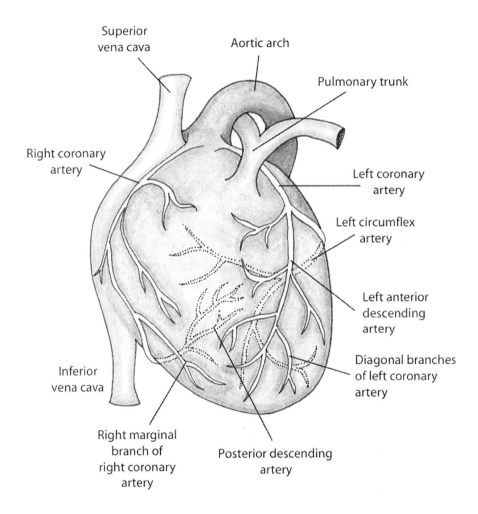

Figure 10: Blood supply to the heart

6: Oesophagus

What is the length of the oesophagus, and what is the distance from incisor to the cardia?

The oesophagus begins beyond the cricoid cartilage and ends at the cardia of the stomach. The distance from incisor to the gastro-oesophageal junction is 40cm, with the oesophagus itself measuring 25cm.

Knowledge of the length is vital for a number of invasive procedures, such as endoscopy, naso-gastric tube placement and insertion of a Sengstaken-Blakemore tube.

What is the blood supply and venous drainage of the oesophagus?

To define the blood supply and drainage of the oesophagus, it is best the divide it into upper, middle and lower segments.

Upper oesophagus:
- Supplied by the inferior thyroid artery from the thyrocervical trunk
- Drainage is into the brachiocephalic vein

Middle oesophagus:
- Supplied by oesophageal branches arising directly from the descending aorta
- Drainage into the azygous vein

Lower oesophagus:
- Supplied by the left gastric artery from the coeliac trunk
- Drainage into the left gastric vein

7: Breast

What are the boundaries of the breast?

Breast size varies greatly, however the margins are relatively constant. These are:

- *Superiorly* – 2nd rib border
- *Inferiorly* – 6th rib border
- *Medially* – sternal edge
- *Laterally* – mid-axillary line

The breast overlies pectoralis major, serratus anterior, external oblique and rectus abdominis although variations in breast size will affect this.

What is the composition of the breast?

The breast is made up of fatty and glandular tissue. Within the fat lie 15-20 lobes and ducts which feed into the nipple-areola complex and are separated by fibrous tissue. The mass of the breast is supported by ligaments (Cooper's ligaments) which attach from the deep fascia (beneath the breast) to the dermis of the skin.

Describe the blood supply of the breast?

This is derived from a number of sources:
- Mostly from the axillary artery branches (lateral thoracic artery and acromio-thoracic artery)
- Perforating branches of the internal thoracic artery
- Posterior intercostal arteries (minor role)

What is the lymph drainage of the breast?

- Mostly to axillary lymph nodes (75%) - to anterior, posterior, central, apical and lateral groups
- Internal thoracic lymph node – medial part of the breast
- Small amounts go to the opposite breast and abdominal wall

8: Chest Radiograph

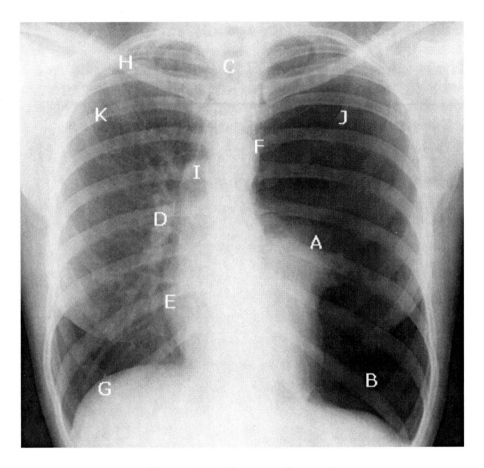

Figure 11: Chest radiograph

What is the pathology seen?

There is a large left-sided pneumothorax, with associated right sided mediastinal shift. No obvious cause for this can be ascertained from the radiograph.

How should this be managed?

Patient will require chest drain insertion on the left side. In the case of tension pneumothorax, formal chest drain insertion should only be performed after needle thoracostomy, as this is a life-threatening illness requiring immediate decompression.

Label the chest radiograph in Figure 11?

A – collapsed right lung

B – absent vascular/lung markings

C – trachea shift to right

D – vascular hilum

E – right atrium

F – aortic notch

G – right hemidiaphragm

H – clavicle

I – mediastinum

J – anterior rib

K – posterior rib

Chapter 3

Head and Neck

1: Skull and Foramina

What is the pterion?

The pterion is the weakest part of the skull, located at the end of the sphenoparietal suture. It is an H-shaped joining of the frontal, parietal, sphenoid and temporal bones.

Its significance comes from the fact that the middle meningeal artery runs on the inner surface past this weak point. Hence, a blow to the side of the head may cause its rupture and subsequently an extra-dural haemorrhage.

The word *pterion* is derived from the Greek meaning 'wings' as it is thought that Hermes, the messenger of the Gods, had his wings attached at his pterion.

What are the divisions of the cranial fossa?

- *Anterior* – extends from the frontal bone to the lesser wings of the sphenoid
- *Middle* – from lesser wings of the sphenoid and clinoid process to petrous part of the temporal bone
- *Posterior* – from the petrous part of the temporal bone to the occipital bone

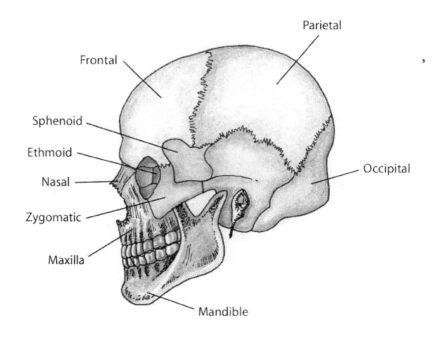

Figure 12: Anatomy of the human skull

In which fossa is the foramen magnum found, and what structures pass through it?

The foramen magnum is located in the posterior cranial fossa, in the occipital bone.

The structures passing through it include:

- Spinal cord (medulla)
- Meninges
- Spinal root of cranial nerve XI
- Vertebral and spinal arteries
- Tectorial membrane
- Alar ligament

2: Venous Sinuses

Describe the drainage of the venous sinuses?

The superior saggital sinus runs along the superior margin of the falx cerebri. The inferior saggital sinus runs along the inferior border of the falx cerebri and connects to the superior saggital sinus via the straight sinus at the 'confluence of the sinuses'. These become the transverse sinus and then the sigmoid sinus. The sigmoid sinus forms the internal jugular vein, once it passes the jugular foramen.

The cavernous sinus is connected to the sigmoid sinus via the superior petrosal sinus and directly to the internal jugular vein via the inferior petrosal sinus.

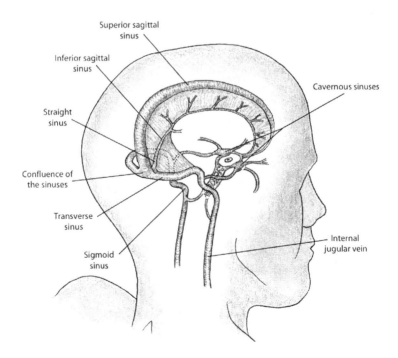

Figure 13: Venous sinuses of the head

What is the cavernous sinus, and where is it located?

- The word cavernous is derived from the Latin meaning 'cave-like'

- The cavernous sinus is a group of thin-walled valveless veins located on either side of the sella turcica. They receive blood from the facial, middle cerebral and sphenoid veins.

What is the clinical relevance of the cavernous sinus and what nerves pass through it?

Notable structures passing through the cavernous sinus include:
- Internal carotid artery
- Cranial nerves III, IV, V^1 and V^2 – passing through the lateral wall of the sinus
- Cranial nerve VI – passing within the substance of the sinus next to the internal carotid artery

Knowledge of anatomy is vital when considering facial and nasal infections as they can spread rapidly via the ophthalmic and facial veins into the cavernous sinus. The sinus is then prone to thrombosis, as well as to systemic sepsis. Pressure on the cranial nerves from obstructed venous drainage (from thrombosis or tumour) may manifest clinically as ophthalmoplegia and sensory loss over the maxilla.

3: Triangles of the neck

Describe the boundaries of the anterior and posterior triangles of the neck?

Anterior triangle:
- *Laterally*   -   anterior border of sternocleidomastoid
- *Medially*   -   midline
- *Superiorly* -   lower border of mandible

Posterior triangle:
- *Laterally*   -   posterior border of sternocleidomastoid
- *Medially*   -   anterior border of trapezius
- *Superiorly* -   clavicle (middle third)

What are the contents of the anterior triangle?

- Vessels   —   Common carotid and bifurcation
                        Jugular veins
                        Facial veins

- Nerves —   Ansa cervicalis
                        Vagus
                        Hypoglossal nerve

- Glands —   Thyroid and Parathyroid
                        Submandibular

- Skeletal —   Trachea
                        Larynx and Hyoid bone

- Lymph nodes

Note – The carotid sheath is located under the anterior border of the sternocleidomastoid and therefore, strictly speaking, not actually a content.

What are the contents of the posterior triangle?

- Vessels – subclavian artery
  suprascapular artery and vein
  external jugular vein
  cervical artery and vein

- Nerves – spinal root of cranial nerve XI
  Trunks of the brachial plexus

- Lymph nodes

4: Mandible

What is the embryological origin of the mandible?

It arises from Meckel's Cartilage, which is from the 1st Branchial arch.

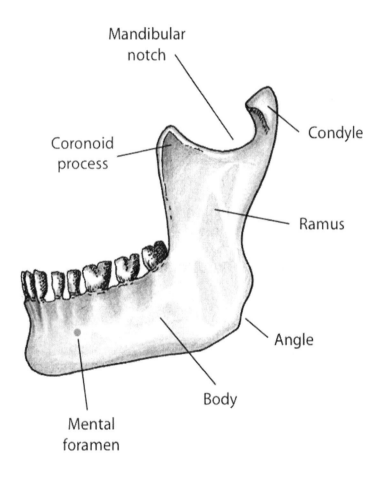

Figure 14: Anatomy of the left mandible
(external side view)

Which muscles are responsible for elevation and depression of the mandible?

Elevation – masseter, temporalis and medial pterygoid muscles

Depression – Medial pterygoid, suprahyoid muscles

Where is the mandibular foramen and what is its clinical significance?

- The mandibular foramen is found on inner border of the rami. Clinically, this is where the inferior alveolar nerve (from the mandibular branch of trigeminal nerve) passes into the mandibular canal. A branch of it can then be seen emerging through the mental foramen, on the outer aspect of the body, known as the mental nerve.

- Knowledge of the nerve's anatomy is used to give nerve blocks.

- Nerve block near the mandibular foramen causes anaesthesia of :

    (a) mandibular teeth to midline – via inferior alveolar nerve

    (b) chin & lower lip – via mental nerve

- The tongue may also become anaesthetised as the lingual nerve is in close proximity to the inferior alveolar nerve.

5: Cranial Blood Supply

Draw a diagram of the circle of Willis.

The circle of Willis describes the anastomosis between the vertebral system and the internal carotid artery.

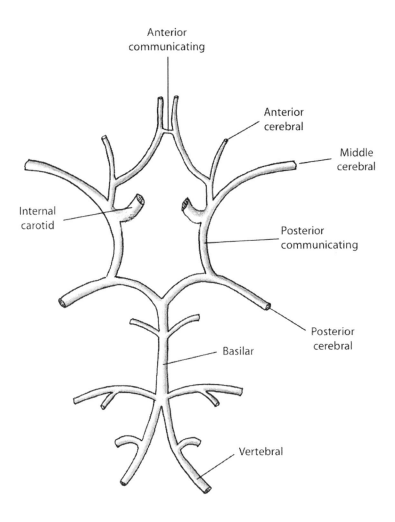

Figure 15: Anatomy of the circle of Willis

Where is the circle of Willis situated?

It is located, and anastomoses around, the pituitary stalk and optic chiasm.

What regions of the brain are supplied by the cerebral vessels?

Anterior cerebral artery – medial and superolateral cerebral hemisphere.

Middle cerebral artery – most of the temporal lobe, the parietal lobe and internal capsule.

Posterior cerebral artery – occipital and inferior temporal regions

How much of the cardiac output is supplied to the brain?

Approximately 20% is delivered to the brain. This is under constant autoregulation so that blood flow remains relatively constant over a wide range of mean arterial pressures.

6: Head and Neck Vessels

What are the branches of the external carotid artery?

The external carotid artery begins at the upper border of the thyroid cartilage (C4) after the bifurcation of the common carotid artery.

The branches of the external carotid artery are:
1. Superior thyroid artery
2. Ascending pharyngeal artery
3. Lingual artery
4. Facial artery
5. Occipital artery
6. Posterior auricular artery
7. Maxillary artery
8. Superficial temporal artery

Describe the path of the vertebral artery?

The two vertebral arteries are derived from the 1st part of the subclavian artery. They then ascend in the neck, each through a small foramen located in the transverse process of vertebra C6-C1. Although C7 also possesses a foramina transversarium, the vertebral arteries do not pass through it. Having traversed C1, the artery passes over the atlas and passes through the foramen magnum. At the level of the medulla, the two vertebral arteries join to form a single basilar artery.

How does the common carotid artery ascend in the neck?

The common carotid artery has differing origins on each side. On the right, it is an upward continuation of the brachiocephalic trunk, whereas on the left it is a direct branch of the aorta. However, their route in the neck is the same. From behind the sternoclavicular joints, they pass towards the head enclosed medially in the carotid sheath. It is at the level of C6 that the carotid may be palpated most easily by compressing it against the anterior tubercle of the C6 vertebra (carotid tubercle of Chassaignac). The artery then continues to the upper border of the thyroid cartilage, where it bifurcates into the internal and external carotid arteries.

7: Muscles of the neck

What muscles are attached to the hyoid bone?

Suprahyoids:

Muscle	Origin	Attachment	Nerve
Digastric (posterior belly)	Digastric groove	Greater horn of hyoid	Facial nerve
Digastric (anterior belly)	Inner surface of mandible	Greater horn of hyoid	Mylohyoid nerve
Stylohyoid	Styloid process	Greater horn and body of hyoid	Facial nerve
Mylohyoid	Mylohyoid line (of mandible)	Body of hyoid	Mylohyoid nerve
Geniohyoid	Genial tubercle	Body of hyoid	Hypoglossal nerve

Note the different nerve supply of the two bellies of digastrics, underlying their different embryological descent. The anterior and posterior belly arise from the 1st and 2nd branchial arches respectively. The two bellies meet as a tendon passing through a fibrous sling which is attached to the hyoid. The muscles themselves are not attached to the hyoid!

Infrahyoids:

Muscle	Origin	Attachment	Nerve
Sternohyoid	Body of hyoid	Manubrium	Ansa cervicalis
Sternothyroid	Greater horn of hyoid	Manubrium	Ansa cervicalis
Thyrohyoid	Greater horn of hyoid	Thyroid cartilage	C1 nerve
Omohyoid	Body of hyoid	Scapula	Ansa cervicalis

What are the attachments and nerve supply of the sternocleidomastoid muscle?

Origin   -   the sternum and the clavicle

Insertion   -   lateral mastoid and occipital bone

The motor supply is from the spinal accessory nerve, while the sensory supply is from the cervical plexus.

8: Thyroid Gland

At what level is the thyroid gland found?

The thyroid gland is a bi-lobed structure joined by a central isthmus which overlies the 2nd and 3rd tracheal rings. The lobes themselves are larger and extend down to the 6th tracheal ring. However, when pathologically enlarged, they may extend much further – deep in to the mediastinum.

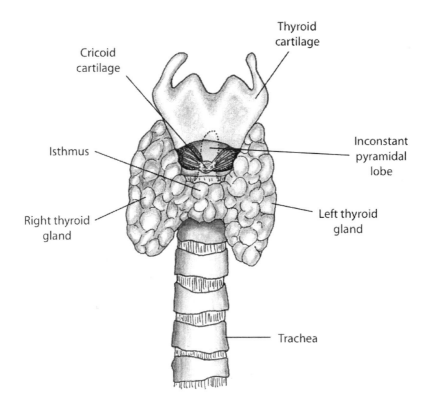

Figure 16: Position of the thyroid gland in the neck

What is the blood supply and venous drainage of the thyroid gland?

It is supplied by:

- Superior thyroid artery - from external carotid artery
- Inferior thyroid artery   - from thyrocervical trunk
- Thyroid Ima Artery   - variable origin
                            - only occurs in 3% of population

Venous drainage is:

- Superior thyroid vein   - into the internal jugular vein
- Middle thyroid vein   - into the internal jugular vein
- Inferior thyroid vein   - into the brachiocephalic veins

What nerves are at risk during thyroidectomy and what is the function of these nerves?

Recurrent laryngeal nerves

Motor   - supplies all muscles of larynx except cricothryoid

Sensory - laryngeal mucosa below level of vocal cords

Superior laryngeal nerve

Motor   - cricothryoid muscle (external branch of nerve)

Sensory - laryngeal mucosa to level of vocal cords
            (internal branch of nerve)

9: Tongue

What are the muscles of the tongue?

The muscles of the tongue can be divided into intrinsic (within the substance of the tongue) and extrinsic (outside but acting on the tongue).

Intrinsic muscles *(alter shape of the tongue)*

- Superior longitudinal

- Inferior longitudinal

- Transverse

- Vertical

Extrinsic muscles *(move the tongue)*

- Genioglossus
  - from genial tubercle to tongue
  - protrusion

- Styloglossus
  - from styloid process to tongue
  - retraction

- Palatoglossus
  - from palatine aponeurosis to tongue
  - elevation

- Hyoglossus
  - from greater horn of hyoid to tongue
  - depression

What is the lymph drainage of tongue?

- *Anterior 2/3* - to the submandibular nodes
- *Posterior 1/3* - to the deep cervical nodes
- *Tip of tongue* - to the submental nodes

What is the nerve supply to the tongue?

When considering enervation of the tongue, it is convenient to talk about the motor supply, sensation and taste.

Motor – all muscles are supplied by the hypoglossal nerve except palatoglossus which is supplied from the pharyngeal plexus (of vagus nerve)

Sensation – the anterior 2/3 is supplied by the lingual nerve (from the mandibular branch of the trigeminal nerve) and the posterior 1/3 is supplied by the glossopharyngeal nerve

Taste – the anterior 2/3 is supplied by the chordae tympani (after joining with facial nerve) and the posterior 1/3 is supplied by the glossopharyngeal nerve

10: Pharyngeal (Branchial) Arches

Describe the pharyngeal arches and what are derived from them?

1st arch (mandibular arch):

Muscle - muscles of mastication
- anterior belly of digastric
- mylohyoid
- two tensor muscles

Skeletal - Meckel's cartilage
- maxilla
- mandible
- incus
- malleus

Enervation - trigeminal nerve CN V^3

2nd arch (Hyoid or Reichert's arch):

Muscle - muscles of facial expression
- posterior belly of digastric
- stylohiod
- stapedius

Skeletal - stapes
- styloid
- stylohyoid
- hyoid (lesser horn)

Enervation - facial nerve CN VII

3rd arch:

Muscle - stylopharyngeus

Skeletal - hyoid (greater horn and body)

Enervation - glossopharyngeal CN IX

4th arch and 6th arch

Muscle - muscle of the larynx, pharynx and palate

Skeletal - thyroid
          - cricoid
          - epiglottic and arytenoids cartilages

Enervation - vagus nerve CN X

Note - The 4th & 6th arches are usually grouped as their mesodermal masses fuse together, thus becoming indistinguishable.

5th arch:

Disappears during development.

Chapter 4

Limb Anatomy

1: Brachial Plexus

What forms the brachial plexus?

The brachial plexus is formed by the union of the ventral rami of nerve roots C5 to C8 and T1, which pass through the gap between the scalenus anterior and medius, along with the subclavian artery.

What is the anatomy of the brachial plexus?

The ventral rami of these nerve *roots* form the *trunks*:
- Superior trunk   - C5 and C6
- Middle trunk   - C7
- Inferior trunk   - C8 and T1

Each *trunk* then divides into the anterior and posterior *divisions*, which form the *cords:*
- Lateral cord   - anterior divisions of the superior and middle trunk
- Medial cord   - anterior division of the inferior trunk
- Posterior cord - posterior divisions of all three trunks

The cords lie lateral, medial and posterior to the second part of the axillary artery.

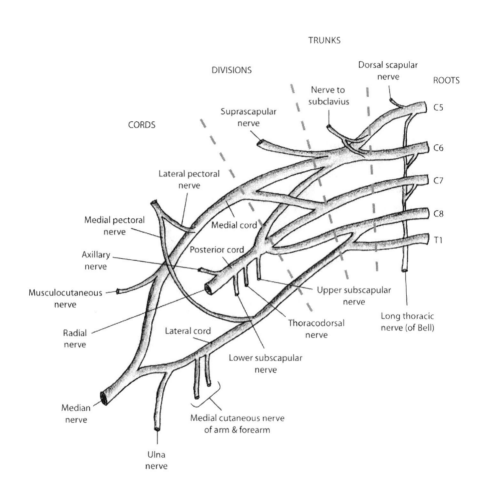

Figure 17: Anatomy of the brachial plexus

Which are the supraclavicular branches of the brachial plexus?

Dorsal scapular nerve	Supplies rhomboids and the levator scapulae (variable)
Long thoracic nerve	Supplies serratus anterior. Also called the Nerve of Bell. Injury leads to winging of the scapula.
Nerve to subclavius	Supplies subclavius and sternoclavicular joint
Suprascapular nerve	Supplies supraspinatus, infraspinatus and the shoulder joint

Which are the infraclavicular branches of the brachial plexus?

From the lateral cord (C5 - C7):

Lateral pectoral nerve	Pectoralis major and branch to pectoralis minor
Musculocutaneous nerve	Coracobrachialis, biceps brachii and brachialis. Sensory supply as lateral cutaneous nerve of forearm.

From the medial cord (C8 and T1):

Ulnar nerve	- Flexor carpi ulnaris - Ulnar half of flexor digitorum profundus - Most muscles of the hand - Skin of the hand medial to a line bisecting the 4th digit (ring finger)

From the medial cord (C8 and T1): Continued

Medial pectoral nerve	Pectoralis minor and part of pectoralis major
Median nerve:	- Flexor muscles of the forearm (except FCU and ulna half of FDP) - Muscles of the hand (abductor, opponens and extensor pollices, and lateral two lumbricals)

Medial cutaneous nerve of arm

Medial cutaneous nerve of forearm

From the posterior cord (C5 - T1) :

Axillary nerve	Deltoid, teres minor and skin over inferior part of deltoid
Radial nerve	- Triceps brachii, anconeus, brachioradialis - Extensor muscles of the forearm - Skin on the posterior aspect of the arm and forearm (posterior cutaneous nerves of arm and forearm)
Upper subscapular	Subscapularis (superior portion)
Lower subscapular	Subscapularis (inferior portion) Teres minor
Thoracodorsal	Latissmus dorsi

What are upper brachial plexus injuries?

Injury to the C5 and C6 spinal nerve roots

Causes: excessive increase in the angle between the neck and the shoulder (e.g. fall onto shoulder or excessive stretching of the neck of a new-born during delivery)

Paralysis of deltoid, biceps, brachialis and brachioradialis occurs, along with sensory loss over the lateral aspect of the upper limb

The clinical picture is an upper limb with an adducted shoulder, medially rotated arm and extended elbow (waiter's tip position)

Also called Erb's palsy, Duchenne's palsy, Duchenne-Erb palsy and upper radicular syndrome

Backpacker's palsy: muscle weakness and cramps in a similar distribution due to stretching of the upper part of the brachial plexus in hikers carrying heavy backpacks for long periods

What are the injuries to the inferior part of the brachial plexus?

Lower brachial plexus injuries occur when the upper limb is suddenly pulled superiorly, injuring the inferior trunk or avulsing the C8 and T1 spinal nerve roots from the spinal cord.

Causes:
- When a person grasps something to break a fall
- During a breech delivery, if the upper limbs are extended and the trunk is pulled forcibly

The clinical picture is that of a claw hand due to paralysis of the small muscles of the hand, also known as Klumpke's palsy.

2: Nerves to the Upper Limb

Describe the course of the axillary nerve?

The axillary nerve is one of the terminal branches of the posterior cord of the brachial plexus. It passes posteriorly and enters the quadrangular space, where it is related to the medial aspect of the surgical neck of the humerus.

It gives off a branch to the shoulder joint and terminates by dividing into an anterior branch and a posterior branch. The anterior branch supplies the deltoid and the skin over its lower half, and the posterior branch supplies the teres minor and continues as the upper lateral cutaneous nerve of the arm.

What are the causes of injury to the axillary nerve?

- Dislocation of the humeral head

- Fracture of the surgical neck of the humerus

- A badly adjusted crutch pressing upwards into the axilla

What is the clinical picture caused by injury to the axillary nerve?

Damage to the axillary nerve leads to paralysis of the deltoid and teres minor muscles, and loss of sensation over the lower half of the deltoid as the upper lateral cutaneous nerve of the arm is practically functionless. Abduction of the arm is impaired, as the deltoid is the main muscle responsible for this function. There is wasting of the deltoid and the greater tuberosity can be readily palpated. Paralysis of the teres minor is not clinically detectable.

Describe the course of the radial nerve?

The radial nerve is the largest branch of the posterior cord of the brachial plexus. It courses posterior to the axillary artery, giving off its motor (long and medial head of triceps) and sensory (posterior cutaneous nerves of the arm) branches. It then lies in the spiral groove supplying the lateral head of triceps and anconeus, giving off the lower lateral cutaneous nerve of the arm and the posterior cutaneous nerve of the forearm.

After emerging on the lateral aspect of the arm in the spiral groove, it enters the anterior compartment of the arm and gives off branches to the brachialis, brachioradialis and the extensor carpi radialis longus. In the cubital fossa it gives off the deep branch of the radial nerve and continues as the superficial radial nerve, which supplies the skin over the lateral half of the dorsum of the hand and the dorsal surface of the lateral two-and-a-half fingers. The deep branch supplies the muscles in the extensor compartment.

The radial nerve is commonly damaged in the axilla, and in the spiral groove.

What are the causes of injury to the radial nerve in the axilla?

- Badly fitted crutch pressing into the axilla

- Falling asleep with one arm over the back of a chair

- Fractures involving the proximal part of the humerus

- Dislocations of the shoulder joint, which stretches the radial nerve

What is the clinical presentation following injury to the radial nerve in the axilla?

Motor:

Paralysis of triceps, anconeus and the long extensors of the wrist leads to loss of extension of the elbow, wrist and fingers. Unopposed action of the flexors leads to wrist drop. Brachioradialis and supinator muscles are also paralysed but supination is still performed by the biceps.

Sensory:

Loss of sensation over a thin strip along the posterior aspect of the arm and the forearm along with loss of sensation over the lateral half of the dorsum of the hand and the lateral two-and-a-half digits.

What are the causes and effect of injury to the radial nerve in the spiral groove?

Causes:

- Fractures of the shaft of the humerus

- Pressure on the back of the arm on the edge of the operating table in an unconscious patient

Clinical picture:

- *Motor:* Wrist drop

- *Sensory:* Loss in the area of distribution in the hand (described above)

What are the causes and result of injury to the deep branch of the radial nerve?

Causes:

- Fractures of the proximal end of the radius
- Dislocation of the radial head

Clinical picture:

- *Motor:* Inability to extend the fingers, but wrist drop does not occur because the extensor carpi radialis longus is preserved.
- *Sensory:* this branch is a motor branch, no sensory loss occurs

Describe the course of the median nerve?

The median nerve arises from the medal and lateral cords of the brachial plexus. It does not give out any branches in the axilla or the arm.

In the cubital fossa, it passes medial to the brachial artery and the biceps tendon. It supplies the muscles of the flexor compartment in the forearm, except the flexor carpi ulnaris and the medial half of the flexor digitorum profundus.

It crosses the wrist below the flexor retinaculum, between the tendons of flexor carpi radialis and flexor digitorum superficialis, overlapped by that of palmaris longus.

In the hand it supplies the muscles of the thenar eminence and the lateral two lumbricals. The palmar cutaneous branch arises in the forearm and crosses superficial to the flexor retinaculum, and supplies the skin on the lateral half of the palm and the lateral three-and-a-half fingers.

The median nerve most commonly gets injured at the elbow or the wrist.

What are the causes and result of median nerve injury at the elbow?

Causes:
Supracondylar fractures of the humerus

Clinical picture:
Motor:
- Loss of pronation at the elbow. The forearm is kept supinated.
- Loss of flexion at the wrist and ulnar deviation, due to greater strength of flexor carpi ulnaris than radialis
- On making a fist, loss of flexion of the interphalangeal joints of the index and middle fingers and weakness of those of the ring and little fingers (ulnar half of flexor digitorum profundus, supplied by the ulnar nerve, remains intact). The metacarpophalangeal joints are still flexed to some extent by the dorsal interoseii.
- Loss of flexion, abduction and opposition of the thumb, along with wasting of the thenar eminence. Ape-like thumb.

Sensory:
- Sensory loss over the lateral aspect of the palm as well as the palmar surface of the lateral three-and–a-half digits.

Vasomotor
- Areas involved in sensory loss are warmer and drier than normal because of arteriolar dilation, and loss of sweating due to loss of sympathetic supply.

Trophic:
- In long-standing cases, the skin becomes dry and scaly. The nails become brittle, and atrophy of the pulp of the fingers occurs.

What are the causes and effects of injury to the median nerve at the wrist?

Causes:
- Carpal tunnel syndrome
- Stab wounds or slashing of the wrist

Clinical picture:
- Paralysis and wasting of the muscles of the thenar eminence of the hand and an ape-like thumb
- Sensory loss in the hand, in the distribution described above
- Vasomotor and trophic changes, as described above.

Describe the course of the ulnar nerve?

The ulnar nerve arises from the medial cord of the brachial plexus. It gives off no branches in the axilla or the arm.

It enters the forearm behind the medial epicondyle, and supplies the flexor carpi ulnaris and the medial half of flexor digitorum profundus.

In the distal part of the forearm, it gives off the palmar and posterior cutaneous branches, which together supply the medial one-third of the skin of the hand and the medial one-and-a-half fingers.

It enters the palm by passing superficial to the flexor retinaculum, and supplies all the muscles of the hand except those of the thenar eminence and the lateral two lumbricals.

The ulnar nerve is most commonly injured at the elbow and the wrist.

What are the causes and the result of damage to the ulnar nerve at the elbow?

Cause:

Fractures involving the medial epicondyle

Clinical picture:

- *Claw hand:* there is extension at the metacarpophalangeal joints and flexion at the interphalangeal joints of the medial two fingers. This occurs due to paralysis of the medial two lumbricals.

- *Inability to adduct the thumb:* if the patient is asked to grip a piece of paper between the thumb and the index finger, they do so by contracting the flexor pollicis longus and by flexing the terminal phalanx (Froment's sign).

- *Inability to adduct or abduct the fingers,* and hence an inability to grip a piece of paper between the fingers.

- *Paralysis of flexor carpi ulnaris:* this causes abduction of the wrist on flexing it. Also, the tendon does not become taut while passing through the pisiform bone.

- *Paralysis of flexor digitorum profundus:* this causes inability to flex the medal two fingers completely.

- *Wasting of the hypothenar eminence*

- *Sensory loss* in the area of distribution of the ulnar nerve in the hand (as described above)

- *Trophic and vasomotor changes* (as described above)

What is the result of ulnar nerve damage at the wrist?

In the wrist, the ulnar artery is commonly damaged at the point where it is superficial to the flexor retinaculum, often due to cuts and stab wounds.

Clinical picture:

- *Claw hand* is much more obvious because flexor digitorum profundus is intact and causes marked flexion of the phalanges

- *Inability to adduct the thumb*

- *Inability to adduct or abduct the digits*

- *Wasting of the hypothenar eminence*

- *Sensory loss*: the posterior cutaneous branch usually arises slightly proximal to the wrist and may be spared. Hence, the sensory loss usually involves the palmar aspect of the hand, as described above, and the dorsal aspect is spared.

- *Trophic* and *vasomotor* changes as described above.

3: Cubital Fossa

What are the boundaries of the cubital fossa?

Superiorly	An imaginary line connecting the medial and lateral epicondyles
Medially	Pronator teres
Laterally	Brachioradialis
Floor	Brachialis and Supinator
Roof	Deep fascia with the bicipital aponeurosis, subcutaneous tissue and skin

What are the contents of the cubital fossa?

Deep structures:
(medially to laterally)

Median nerve

Brachial artery - its terminal part and the commencement of its terminal branches, the radial and ulnar arteries

Deep veins accompanying the arteries

Biceps brachii tendon

Superficial structures:
(in the subcutaneous tissue overlying the fascia)

Median cubital vein - crosses the brachial artery diagonally

Cutaneous nerve

4: Carpal Tunnel

What are the boundaries of the carpal tunnel?

Roof – the flexor retinaculum

Floor – the concave carpus

The flexor retinaculum is a fibrous band which attaches at the scaphoid and trapezium on the radial side, and to the hook of hamate and pisiform on the ulna side.

What are the contents of the carpal tunnel?

The content include:

• Median nerve

• four flexor digitorum superficialis tendons (arranged in pairs)

• four flexor digitorum profundus tendons (arranged in a straight line)

• Flexor pollicis longus (on radial side of FDS)

• Flexor carpii radialis (this travels in its own fascial compartment)

Remember: the ulna nerve and artery pass through Guyon's canal, superiorly and to the ulna side of the flexor retinaculum, and are therefore not within the carpal tunnel.

What nerves are at risk during carpal tunnel decompression?

- Median nerve

- Palmar cutaneous branch (of median nerve)
    - sensory supply to skin of thenar eminence
    - runs superficial to the flexor retinaculum

- Recurrent motor branch (of median nerve)
    - found toward the radial border, supplying the thenar muscles
    - although uncommon, injury to this nerve has much greater clinical consequence

- Ulna nerve

- Ulna and radial artery

5: Hip and Femur

What are the anatomical considerations of proximal femoral fractures?

The hip joint is a ball and socket synovial joint, between the head of the femur and the acetabulum. The capsule of the joint is attached around the acetabular labrum and passes laterally to the femoral neck. Anteriorly it attaches to the intertrochanteric line, but posteriorly it only extends half the distance of the neck to the intertrochanteric line. Understanding the blood supply to the femoral head is crucial to the management of these fractures.

The extracapsular arterial ring at the base of the femoral neck is formed by contributions from the medial and lateral femoral circumflex arteries. Ascending cervical branches contribute to a subsynovial intra-articular ring. The artery of the ligament of teres contributes very little to the blood supply of the femoral head. To summarise, the blood supply to the head of the femur is from capsular, intramedullary and ligamentum teres vessels.

How are these fractures classified?

Broadly speaking, proximal femoral fractures include fractures of the femoral neck and trochanteric fractures. However, an important distinction needs to be made between intracapsular versus extracapsular fractures. The former can severely compromise the vascular supply to the head of the femur, leading to malunion or avascular necrosis. This key concept governs the principles of management.

Garden's classification of femoral neck fractures

1. Impacted / incomplete
2. Complete with slight displacement, has trabecular continuity
3. Complete displaced, loss of trabecular continuity
4. Complete fracture with full displacement, but trabecular continuity maintained

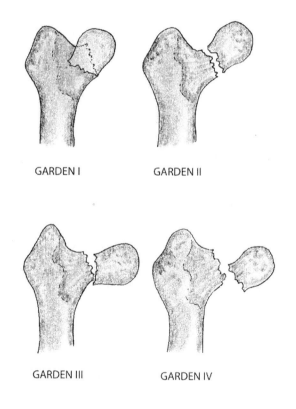

Figure 18: The Garden classification of femoral neck fractures on AP view

What is the management of these fractures?

Operative treatment is almost mandatory. Pain relief, return to mobility and prevention of both bedsores and pulmonary complications are the usual indications.

Undisplaced and impacted intracapsular fractures can be conservatively managed by protected weight-bearing but regular radiographs to detect displacement are needed.

Displaced intracapsular fractures can be treated by internal fixation with cannulated screws. However, they often require prosthetic replacement of the femoral head with a hemiarthroplasty (Austin Moore, Thompson or bipolar prostheses), or total hip replacement.

Intertrochanteric fractures unite very well but are unstable, and malunion is common unless they are internally fixed. This is normally with the use of a dynamic hip screw or and intra-medullary hip screw.

What are the major complications?

1. The mortality for these fractures is approximately 10% at six weeks and 30% within one year.
2. Osteoarthritis
3. Avascular necrosis
4. Malunion

6: Adductor Canal of Hunter

What are the boundaries of the adductor canal?

Roof and anteromedially – sartorius
(as it runs obliquely over the leg)

Floor – adductor longus and magnus

Anterolaterally – vastus medialis

The adductor canal commences at the apex of the femoral triangle and ends at the adductor hiatus (which is the opening in the adductor magnus muscle). The adductor hiatus marks the end of the femoral artery and vein, as they pass into the popliteal fossa.

Interestingly, the saphenous nerve does not complete its journey through the canal. Instead, it pierces through the fibres of sartorius and gracilis before reaching the adductor hiatus. It passes medial to the knee and descends into the lower leg in close proximity to the long saphenous vein, supplying sensation to a thin strip of skin extending down to the foot.

What are the contents of the adductor canal?

- Femoral artery and vein

- Saphenous nerve

- Nerve to vastus medialis

- Occasionally has genicular branches to the knee

7: Knee Joint

What are the articulations in the knee joint?

The knee is the largest joint in the body and is classified as a hinge joint.

It is made up of 2 separate articulations:
- femur and tibia
- femur and patella

Describe the main ligaments and other soft tissues in and around the knee joint?

Collateral ligaments
- Medial (tibial) and lateral (fibular) collateral ligaments
- Resist valgus and varus stresses
- Medial collateral ligament attaches from the medial femoral condyle to the medial tibial condyle and the medial tibia
- Lateral collateral ligament attaches from the lateral femoral condyle to the lateral part of the fibular head
- Extracapsular

Cruciate ligaments
- Anterior and posterior cruciate ligaments
- Resist backwards and forward displacement of the femur
- Named for their cross-like attachments at the tibial plateau
- Anterior cruciate ligament attaches anterior on the tibial spine, and crosses upwards and backwards to attach at the medial part of the lateral femoral condyle
- Posterior cruciate ligament attaches posterior on the tibial spine, and crosses upwards and forwards to attach at the lateral part of the medial femoral condyle
- Intracapsular

Patellar ligament
- Attaches just below the tibial tuberosity
- Can be thought of as a continuation of the quadriceps tendon
- Strengthens the capsule anteriorly

Menisci:
- Medial and lateral menisci
- Act to absorb shock through the knee joint
- Crescent-shaped fibrocartilages
- Medial meniscus attaches at its inner surface to the tibial plateau (between the condyles). The periphery attaches to the capsule of the joint, as well as to the medial collateral ligament
- Lateral meniscus also attaches to the tibial plateau (between the condyles) on its inner surface. However, its periphery cannot attach to the capsule of lateral collateral ligament due to the presence of the popliteus tendon

What do you understand by the term 'locking and unlocking of the knee'?

Locking of the knee occurs on standing and weight-bearing through the knee. The weight of the body is transmitted directly through the joint so that the quadriceps and hamstring muscles are largely relaxed. This allows energy saving without compromising stability.

When standing, the femur rotates medially onto the tibia, thus screwing it into a fixed position. To unlock the knee, popliteus contracts to bring the alignment back to normal (femur rotates laterally on tibia). Only after this has occurred, can the hamstrings act to bring about flexion of the knee, thus unscrewing it.

8: Popliteal Fossa

What are the boundaries of the popliteal fossa?

The popliteal fossa is diamond-shaped, and situated on the posterior aspect of the knee joint.

The popliteal fossa is bound by:

Laterally: The biceps femoris above, and the lateral head of gastrocnemius and plantaris below

Medially: The semi-membranosus and semi-tendinosus above and the medial head of gastrocnemius below

The *floor* of the popliteal fossa is formed by the popliteal surface of the femur, the oblique popliteal ligament of the knee joint and the popliteus.

The *roof* of the popliteal fossa is formed by fascia and skin.

What are the contents of the popliteal fossa?

In order, deep to superficial:

- Popliteal artery
- Popliteal vein
- Tibial nerve and the common peroneal nerve

The fossa also contains:

- the short saphenous vein
- the posterior cutaneous nerve of the thigh
- the popliteal lymph nodes and lymphatics.

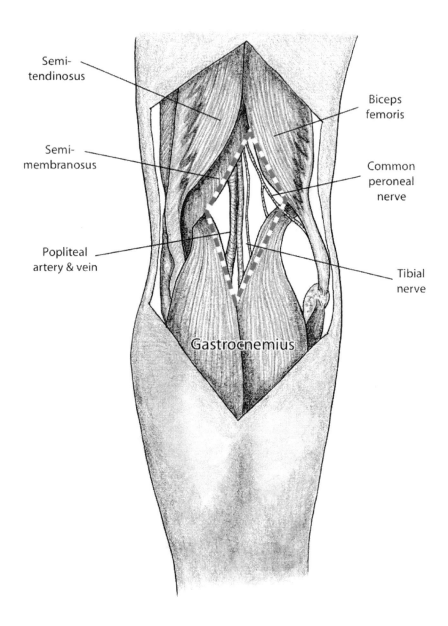

Figure 19: The popliteal fossa and its contents

9: Ankle

What are the anatomical aspects of the ankle relevant to its injury?

The ankle joint is a modified hinge synovial joint. Articular surfaces include the talus and distal tibia, stabilised by the medial and lateral malleoli and strengthened by surrounding ligaments. Fracture of the ankle can lead to the combined damage of both bony and soft tissue structures.

Important considerations are listed below:
* Medial, lateral and posterior malleoli
* Tibiofibular syndesmosis
* Deltoid (medial collateral) ligament
* Tibial plafond
* Talar position
* Lateral ligaments (calcaneofibular)
                      (anterior/posterior talofibular)

What are the mechanisms of and patterns of injury associated with the ankle?

1. Abduction - Lateral malleolar fracture
              - Deltoid rupture
              - Medial malleolar fracture

2. Adduction - Partial tear of anterior inferior talofibular ligament
              - Lateral collateral ligament rupture
              - Lateral malleolar avulsion

3. External rotation - Deltoid ligament rupture
                      - medial malleolus avulsion, with severe damage to lateral side and possibility of posterior malleolar fracture

4. Axial compression - Damage to the tibial plafond

How are ankle fractures classified?

Weber Classification

Type A – Fracture below the inferior tibiofibular syndesmosis
Type B – Fracture at the level of the syndesmosis
Type C – Fracture above the syndesmosis

Lauge Hansen – Based on mechanism of injury to determine best method of reduction.

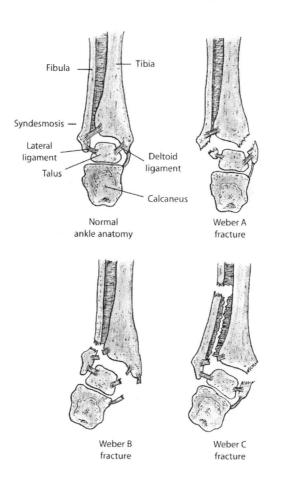

Figure 20: The Weber classification for ankle fractures

What imaging is necessary for diagnosis and classification?

Three X-ray views are ideal
- Anteroposterior
- Lateral
- Mortise view (30° oblique projection of inferior tibiofibular joint)

What are the principles of management?

1. Although rare, neurovascular injury should be ruled out.
2. Early reduction of subluxation/dislocation followed by splintage, elevation and ice.
3. Accurate anatomical reduction and stabilisation.
4. The key to stability is the Weber classification. Weber A fractures are usually stable once malleolar fracture reduction has been achieved. This is usually by plaster cast. Weber C fractures commonly require internal fixation. Diastasis should be reduced.
5. Isolated medial malleolar fractures, if undisplaced, can be managed conservatively. If the medial malleolar fragment involves a large proportion of the articular surface, ORIF with screws is recommended.
6. For undisplaced bi-malleolar fractures below the syndesmosis, plaster immobilisation is satisfactory. Displaced fractures and fracture dislocations require anatomical reduction and internal fixation.
7. Post-operatively a below-knee cast is required, and the patient allowed to partial weight-bear.

What are the common complications?

- Stiffness
- Osteoarthritis
- Complex regional pain syndrome

10: Compartments of the Leg

How are the compartments formed and how many are there?

The deep fascia of the leg, intermuscular septa and the interosseous membrane divide the leg into three compartments:
- Anterior compartment
- Lateral compartment
- Posterior compartment

Describe the contents of the anterior compartment?

Muscles:　　　　　Tibialis anterior
　　　　　　　　　Extensor digitorum longus
　　　　　　　　　Peroneus tertius
　　　　　　　　　Extensor hallucis longus

Blood supply:　　Anterior tibial artery

Nerve supply:　　Deep peroneal nerve

What are the contents of the lateral compartment?

Muscles:　　　　　Peroneus longus
　　　　　　　　　Peroneus brevis

Blood supply:　　Branches from the peroneal artery

Nerve supply:　　Superficial peroneal nerve

What are the contents of the posterior compartment?

The posterior compartment is split into deep and superficial by the deep transverse fascia of the leg.

Superficial muscle group: Gastrocnemius
Plantaris
Soleus

Deep muscle group: Popliteus
Flexor digitorum longus
Flexor hallucis longus
Tibialis posterior

Blood supply: Posterior tibial artery

Nerve supply: Tibial nerve

What is compartment syndrome?

Increased pressure in a fascial compartment leading to impairment of venous drainage. This results in oedema with resultant ischaemia, leading to cell death.

What can cause compartment syndrome?

- Fractures (especially proximal tibia, forearm and elbow)
- Burns
- Plaster casts
- Haemorrhage
- Infection
- Post-operative (internal fixation)
- Decreased serum osmolality (e.g. nephritic syndrome)

How can compartment syndrome be diagnosed?

The classic features of ischaemia include :

Pain

Paraesthesia

Pulselessness

Pallor

Paralysis

In compartment syndrome the earliest features are pain on passive stretch and altered sensibility. The presence of a pulse does not exclude the diagnosis.

It is possible to measure intra-compartmental pressure. Opinions vary, but one school of thought advocates that if the difference between the diastolic blood pressure and the pressure measured within the compartment is less than 30mmHg, then this is an indication for urgent treatment. However, clinical judgment is of paramount importance.

How is compartment syndrome treated?

Compartment syndrome is a surgical emergency. The compartment must be urgently decompressed. All casts and bandages must be removed, not merely split, and the limb nursed flat.

In the case of the leg, fasciotomy means decompression of all four compartments through long medial and lateral incisions. The wounds are left open and revisited in forty-eight hours for inspection, debridement, suturing or skin-grafting.

Part 2

Critical Care

1: Sepsis

What is systemic inflammatory response syndrome (SIRS) and how is it characterised?

SIRS is the body's response to an insult which results in a non-specific inflammatory response.

It is characterised by 2 or more of:

- Temp > 38°C or < 36°C
- Pulse rate > 90 bpm
- Respiratory rate > 20/min or P_aCO_2 < 4.3kPa (32mmHg)
- WCC > 12 or < 4, or >10% immature forms

What is septic shock?

Septic shock occurs along the spectrum of sepsis where there is refractory hypotension, despite adequate fluid administration, which results in cellular hypoperfusion. This can be detected clinically in a number of ways such as a low systolic BP, high lactate level or oliguria. The mortality from septic shock ranges from 28-50% or more.

What is multi-organ dysfunction syndrome (MODS)?

MODS is defined as the failure of 2 or more organ systems, such that bodily homeostasis can no longer be regulated without external influence. Interestingly, MODS was initially described in ruptured aortic aneurysm patients, but descriptions from a variety of causes soon followed, in particular sepsis.

How do you manage a patient with septic shock and what are the main principles?

In 2001, the *New England Journal of Medicine* published comprehensive guidelines on early goal-directed therapy in septic shock, which many hospitals have since accepted as part of their protocol.

Basic principles include:

- Supplemental Oxygen therapy (aim to keep central venous sats > 70%)
- mechanical ventilation if necessary
- IV access & central line.
- Fluid resuscitate (10-20mls per kg as bolus)
- Send bloods including FBC, U&E, clotting, G&S and blood cultures
- Catheterise and maintain urine output to >0.5mls/kg/hour
- Start empirical antibiotic therapy, within 1 hour where possible but only after blood cultures have been obtained
- Inotropes and vasopressors if mean arterial pressure is >65 mmHg
- Manage patients in HDU or ICU setting

Newer guidelines from *Intensive Care Medicine* (2004) added

- Use of activated protein C for high risk patients with septic shock, MODS or ARDS associated with sepsis
- Target Hb of 7.0 – 9.0 g/dl
- Meticulous glycaemic control <8.3mmol/l

2: Pulmonary Artery Catheter

Draw the changes in waveform as you travel from right atrium, to right ventricle, to pulmonary artery, to the wedge pressure?

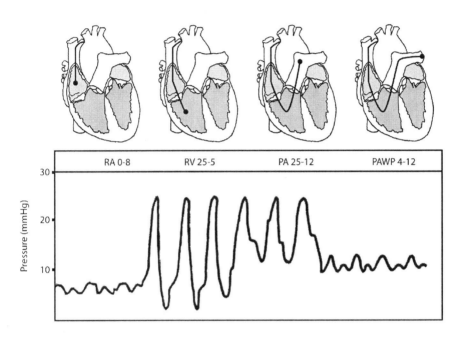

Figure 21: Change of pressure waveform from
right atrium to pulmonary artery

What is a Swann-Ganz catheter?

A Swann-Ganz catheter is a transducing, flow-directed, balloon-tipped pulmonary artery flotation catheter.

What are the indications for a pulmonary artery catheter?

- Management of shock, particularly when more than one type of shock is present
- Measurement of cardiac output
- Post cardiac surgery (in haemodynamically compromised patient)
- Measurement of oxygenation in various chambers of the heart
- Post myocardial infarct (complicated by valvular lesion or septal defect)
- Diagnosis of primary pulmonary hypertension

What values are measured and which are derived from the catheter?

Measured
- Pulmonary artery wedge pressure (PAWP)
- Left atrial pressure (LAP)
- Left ventricular end diastolic pressure (LVEDP)
- Cardiac output
- Cardiac index

Derived
- Systemic vascular resistance
- Pulmonary vascular resistance
- Stroke volume
- O_2 consumption
- Left ventricular stroke work

What assumptions do we make in using a pulmonary catheter?

In order for pulmonary artery wedge pressure (PAWP) to be synonymous with left atrial pressure (LAP) and left ventricular end diastolic pressure (LVEDP), we must assume a continuous standing column of blood from pulmonary artery to the left ventricle, with no pathology between. Therefore patients with pulmonary embolism, mitral valve disease or decreased left ventricular compliance will have inaccurate results.

What complications can occur from insertion of a pulmonary artery catheter?

- Infection (2-15%)

- Arterial puncture

- Pneumothorax (~2%)

- Ventricular rupture

- Pulmonary artery rupture / ischaemia/infarct (<1%)

- Arrhythmias – particularly RBBB (5%)
        (beware in patients with pre-existing LBBB as they may go into complete heart block)

What alternatives to pulmonary artery catheters are you aware of?

- Oesophageal Doppler – measures velocity of flow in descending thoracic aorta and derives cardiac output from this.
- LiDCO (Lithium Dilution Cardiac Output) – Uses chemodilution of lithium over a certain distance to calculate flow.

What is the current evidence for the use of pulmonary artery catheters?

The PACman study (2005) was a single blinded randomised control trial looking at the use of PAC in intensive care units. It found that the use of PACs had no effect on mortality when compared with no PAC use or with an alternative means of calculating cardiac output (CO) in critically ill patients on the ITU. Nevertheless, their use still remains invaluable in specialist tertiary centres.

3: General Anaesthetic

What makes up a general anaesthetic?

The three main components are:
- Hypnotic (e.g. propofol)
- Analgesic (e.g. morphine)
- Muscle relaxant (e.g. atracurium)

What types of muscle relaxants are you aware of, and what is the difference in their mechanism of action?

There are two main types of muscle relaxant:
- Depolarising
- Non-depolarising

Depolarising (e.g. suxamethonium)
- Acts at the motor end plate to stop signal transduction by binding to the Ach receptors which they activate
- Reverses spontaneously after a few minutes due to the action of an intrinsic enzyme called plasma cholinesterase. (Beware of patients with cholinesterase deficiency as the muscle relaxant may last for up to twenty-four hours!)
- Causes increase in K^+ levels
- Inhibitors are non-competitive

Non-depolarising (e.g. atracurium, vecuronium)
- As their name suggests, they bind to Ach receptors but do not activate them
- Reversed by the action of neostigmine (Patients are usually given glycopyrrolate to counteract cardiac side effects)
- Inhibitors are competitive

4: Local Anaesthetic

What is the mechanism of action of all local anaesthetics?

They work by decreasing voltage-gated Na^+ channel opening and thereby prevent the threshold for depolarisation from occurring.

What are the maximum doses, with and without adrenaline, of bupivocaine, lignocaine and prilocaine?

Bupivocaine	2 mg/kg	2 mg/kg (with adrenaline)
Lignocaine	3 mg/kg	7 mg/kg (with adrenaline)
Prilocaine	6 mg/kg	9 mg/kg (with adrenaline)

These differences arise from the decreased absorption of local anaesthetic which results from local vasoconstriction induced by the adrenaline. *Remember, never use local anaesthetic with adrenaline on an extremity as there is a risk of distal ischaemia/ infarction.*

What are the signs of local anaesthetic toxicity?

- Oral tingling / paraesthesia
- Cardiac dysrhythmias
- Muscular excitability
- Convulsions
- Prilocaine may cause methaemaglobinaemia

- Tinnitus
- Drowsiness
- Coma
- Death

How do you treat local anaesthetic toxicity?

Correct calculation of doses should be performed before administration of any local anaesthetic, to ensure a safe dose is given.

However, if signs of toxicity develop, make sure that the patient is managed as a medical emergency:

- ABC
- Full monitoring, including cardiac monitoring
- May need oxygen supplementation
  (for example, if convulsing, the patient may require an airway adjunct, such as a nasopharyngeal airway)
- Treat any dysrhythmias appropriately
- Treat convulsions with anticonvulsants
- Definitive treatment for cardiotoxicity can be achieved by use of IV lipid infusion to bind up the anaesthetic, especially when cardiac manifestations occur
- In rare circumstances, and where available, cardiopulmonary bypass has also been used

What other uses are there for local anaesthetics in medicine?

Local anaesthetics are also Vaughn Williams Class I antiarrhythmics. Lignocaine is therefore used in the treatment of ventricular tachyarrhthmias

5: Cardiac Tamponade

What is the difference between a pericardial effusion and a cardiac tamponade?

Pericardial effusion is the presence of fluid in the pericardial sac, whereas cardiac tamponade occurs when there is diastolic collapse. It is best to consider them as clinical events spanning the same spectrum although pericardial effusions are classically associated with chronic clinical conditions such as rheumatoid arthritis.

How may a patient with acute cardiac tamponade present?

Cardiac tamponade is a medical emergency. Patient usually presents with cardiac arrest (pulseless electrical activity). There is also usually a history trauma (often penetrative) to the chest.

What are the clinical signs of cardiac tamponade?

Tamponade is classically described as exhibiting:

- Beck's triad (hypotension, muffled heart sounds, raised JVP)
- Pulsus parodoxus (abnormal rise in blood pressure of more than 10 mmHg)

The clinical picture will also depend upon the speed at which the fluid accumulates. The pericardial sac usually contains about 20-50mls of fluid. A rapid rise to 100mls can be enough to cause tamponade, whereas the slow accumulation of 500mls may leave the patient asymptomatic.

What is the treatment for cardiac tamponade?

- Emergency needle pericardiocentesis is performed by inserting a large-bore needle at the xiphisternum, angled toward the left shoulder tip.

- This procedure should be done under cardiac monitoring, and interference or ST segment elevation is seen on the cardiac monitor when the pericardial sac is entered.

- Continue aspirating with cardiac monitoring until all of the blood has been aspirated, and there is a return of cardiac activity with associated cardiac output.

- Following trauma, tamponade will frequently require emergency surgery to definitively treat the underlying injury.

6: Central Line

What are the indications for central venous access?

- Vascular access where peripheral access has proved unobtainable. It should be noted that a 14G cannula in a large peripheral vein will provide a faster delivery route than a central line. Remember Hagan-Pouseille Law – flow $\propto r^4$

- Central delivery of certain drugs (e.g. amiodarone, thrombolytics and inotropes)

- Central venous pressure monitoring

- Total parenteral nutrition (preferably through a dedicated single lumen catheter)

- Pacing wire insertion

- Central venous oxygenation monitoring (e.g. in sepsis)

- Haemofiltration

Are you aware of any contra-indications to central line insertion?

- Localised infection over the insertion site

- Coagulopathy - this is an absolute contraindication for subclavian access but a relative contraindication for jugular or femoral access

- Inability to tolerate a pneumothorax on the ipsilateral side

- Patient refusal / uncooperative patient

Describe the process of inserting a central line via the internal jugular vein?

Current guidelines advocate the insertion of a central line under ultrasonic guidance when inserting jugular or femoral lines, but not when inserting subclavian lines.

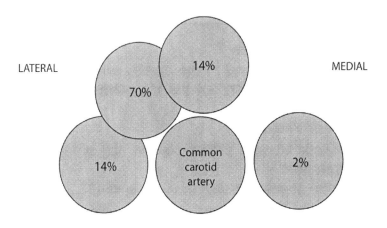

Figure 22: Normal variations in the position of the internal jugular vein

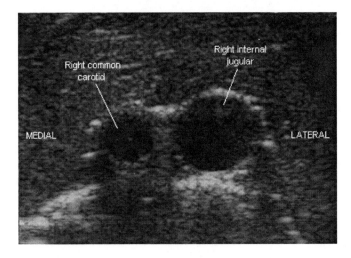

Figure 23: Ultrasound of the showing the relevant anatomy of the right internal jugular

Describe the process of inserting a central line via the internal jugular vein (continued)?

- Aseptic technique should be maintained throughout
- Local anaesthetic is infiltrated
- Palpate the carotid artery
- Insert the needle lateral to the carotid artery, at the level of thyroid cartilage, aiming for the ipsilateral anterior superior iliac spine.
- Aspirate while advancing
- When venous blood is drawn, remove the syringe and insert a Seldinger wire
- Remove the needle, leaving the wire in situ
- Dilate the tract if necessary, and insert a central line catheter over the wire
- Remove the wire and aspirate/flush each port
- Secure the central line by suturing it to the skin
- Post-procedure chest X-ray to locate the tip of the catheter, and to ensure no pneumothorax

7: Tracheostomy

What are the indications for tracheostomy?

- Upper airway obstruction
- Prolonged mechanical ventilation (more comfortable, easier to manage and easier to wean off)
- Neurological diseases of the respiratory tract (e.g. myasthenia gravis)
- Bronchial toilet (help clear bronchial secretions)

Are you aware of any contra-indications to tracheostomy?

Absolute contraindications

- Infection at site of incision
- Coagulopathy

Relative contraindications

- Emergency setting as complication/failure rates are very high
- Also not recommended for those with laryngeal carcinoma where manipulation may cause more harm

Can tracheostomy be placed in children?

Although technically more difficult, and with greater risk of complications, tracheostomies are still indicated in children for the same reasons as in adults.

However surgical cricothyroidotomy is contra-indicated in children under 12 as the trachea isn't fully developed, and tracheostomy leads to a high incidence of subglottic stenosis.

By which routes can one place a tracheostomy?

- Surgical (open)
- Percutaneous (minimally invasive)

Describe the method by which you would insert a surgical tracheostomy?

- Under general anaesthetic, in supine position
- Prep and drape
- Identify landmarks - thyroid cartilage, cricoid cartilage and sternal notch
- Incision can be vertical or horizontal, but must be centered on the 2nd-3rd tracheal ring
- Dissection continues, remaining midline to avoid paratracheal structures and to aid haemostasis
- Maintain meticulous haemostasis throughout procedure
- Retract strap muscles laterally
- Thyroid isthmus may be retracted but it is often divided and ligated
- Create an inferior flap between 2nd and 3rd tracheal cartilages (Bjork Flap), taking care not to puncture the ET balloon
- Ask anaesthetist to deflate and withdraw the ET tube
- Insert tracheostomy tube and connect to ventilator
- Once ventilation shows adequate $ETCO_2$, suture tracheostomy tube to skin
- Skin is not closed, but opposed to prevent subcutaneous emphysema developing

8: Disseminated Intravascular Coagulation

What is the definition of DIC?

- DIC is a pathological systemic disorder in which there is widespread activation of intravascular coagulation.
- Paradoxically, this leads to consumption of clotting factors, and haemorrhage often co-exists.
- Mortality has been described as 30-50%.
- Remember **D**eath **I**s **C**oming

What clinical signs would you expect to see?

Patients are usually very sick due to an underlying cause

Bleeding tendencies, particularly from multiple sites

Important to realise that any system can be affected:
- *CVS* - hypotensive and tachycardic
- *Respiratory* – ARDS
- *GI* - upper or lower GI bleeds
- *Renal* - Renal failure & haematuria
- *Skin* -   purpuric or petechial rash
       - Haematomas and excessive bleeding from skin puncture sites

What blood tests are of importance?

- *FBC* – look for low platelets and anaemia
- *FDP* and *D-dimer* – evidence of fibrinolysis
- *Coagulation* – excessive bleeding times (APPT & PT are usually high, but can be low or normal)

What are the causes of DIC?

- Obstetric causes (commonest cause worldwide) – including eclampsia and amniotic fluid embolus
- Sepsis – particularly Gram Negative
- Trauma and burns
- Massive blood transfusion – when volume transfused is more than total circulating volume of 4.9 litres
- Transfusion reaction
- Malignancy – particularly acute myelocytic leukaemia
- Surgical – pancreatitis

What treatments are you aware of for DIC?

- Always control and treat the underlying cause
- Transfuse blood if severely anaemic
- Replace platelets if necessary
- FFP is also administered to replace coagulation factors consumed during the process
- Cryoprecipate contains Factor VIII, fibrinogen and von Willebrand factor, and may aid clotting
- Activated Protein C and antithrombin can been used to deactivate clotting factors, thereby decreasing the amount of intravascular coagulation occurring
- Patient should be managed on an intensive care unit with advice from a haematologist

9: Renal Failure

What are the causes of renal failure?

Renal failure can be classified as acute, chronic or a combination of both.

Causes are best described by further sub-division:

Pre-renal
- Hypovolaemic shock / dehydration
- Septic shock
- Cardiac dysfunction
- Renal artery disease

Renal
- Acute tubular necrosis
- Glomerulonephritis
- Interstitial nephritis
- Iatrogenic (aminoglycosides, NSAIDs)

Post renal
- Ureteric – stones, compression from tumours
- Bladder – prostatic tumours / enlargement
             – Bladder tumours
             – Neurological disease preventing appropriate emptying of bladder

How do you assess the degree of renal failure?

This can be done in 2 main ways:

Clinically –   assess patient paying particular attention to urine output

Biochemically – serum creatinine & urea, GFR

What are the stages of acute renal failure?

Remember **R I F L E** (coined by Acute Dialysis Quality Initiative)

Risk   *Injury*   *Failure*   *Loss*   *End Stage*

R   ↑ in creatinine by ×1.5   or   ↓ in GFR by 25%
     or   U/O <0.5 ml/hr/kg for 6 hrs

I   ↑ in creatinine by ×2   or   ↓ in GFR by 50%
     or   U/O <0.5 ml/hr/kg for 12 hrs

F   ↑ in creatinine by ×3   or   ↓ in GFR by 75%
     or   U/O <0.3 ml/hr/kg for 24 hrs/ anuria for 12 hours

L   Persistent ARF with loss of kidney function for >4 weeks

E   Loss of kidney function for >3 months

What are the fundamental differences between haemodialysis (HD) and haemofiltration (HF)?

Haemodialysis involves the use of a semi-permeable membrane, which allows the passage of small molecules down a concentration gradient (OSMOTIC GRADIENT). HD is used to restore the body's biochemical homeostasis.

Haemofiltration achieves clearance by forcing blood through a membrane with larger pores than used in HD to allow removal of plasma and dissolved solutes (HYDROSTATIC GRADIENT). The removed fluid is then replaced, but with an overall loss of the solutes. HF is mainly used as an adjunct to HD, but also offers rapid removal of fluid or certain electrolytes (e.g. K+).

Most intensive care units will use HF as it is cardiovascularly more stable, and therefore safer for critically ill patients. It is worth remembering that they may also be used at the same time, with HF as continuous and HD as intermittent.

10: Pneumothorax

How do you classify types of pneumothorax?

- **Simple** – a non-expanding collection of air in the pleura.

- **Open** – a collection of air in the pleura, associated with a breach of the chest wall, such that the pneumothorax communicates with the atmosphere.

- **Tension** – a build-up of air within the pleura with each breath as the air cannot exit. This is a life threatening emergency.

A patient is bought to A&E following an RTA. He is hypoxic and peri-arrest with a mediastinum shifted to the left. What is your management?

- The patient is likely to be suffering from a tension pneumothorax on the right
- Treatment should include immediate needle decompression of the chest, with a wide-bore cannula being inserted into the 2nd intercostals space along the mid-clavicular line, on the side of the pneumothorax
- Air can usually be heard escaping on inserting the cannula
- The cannula should be secured into place, at which point formal assessment of the patient may be carried out
- A chest drain will need to be inserted as part of the definitive treatment

When would you perform a chest X-ray?

Tension pneumothorax is a clinical diagnosis, and not a radiological one. Chest X-ray should therefore only be carried out once the chest drain is in situ.

Describe the procedure for inserting a chest drain?

- Patient is prepared and draped
- Procedure is under aseptic technique
- Site is usually 5th intercostal space in anterior mid-axillary line
- Skin is infiltrated with lidocaine with adrenaline (to help decrease bleeding)
- Always aspirate before injecting
- Infiltrate deeper, to the pleura, until air/fluid is aspirated
- Make incision through the skin with a scalpel
- Begin blunt dissection with either Roberts or Spencer-Wells forceps
- Aim just above the rib to avoid damage to the neurovascular bundle
- Once pleura is opened, ensure the tract is large enough by inserting little finger into pleura and freeing any adhesions
- Chest drain is then inserted, without the trocar, using the forceps as a guide
- Once in situ, chest drain is connected to an under water seal
- Secure chest drain in place by suture and apply dressings
- Perform post-procedure chest X-ray

What layers are traversed during chest drain insertion?

Layers (in order):
- Skin
- Subcutaneous tissue
- External intercostal muscle
- Internal intercostal muscle
- Innermost intercostal muscle
- Parietal pleura

11: Head Injury

What is the Glasgow Coma Scale (GCS)?

The GCS was initially developed in 1974 as a method for assessing and predicting the outcome from head injuries. Its application has since evolved into a way of assessing neurological status in any patient. Perhaps most usefully, it gives a repeatable score, usable by most medical staff, which can follow the patient's progress.

The Glasgow Coma Scale can be summarised as:

Motor

1. No response
2. Extends to pain
3. Flexes to pain
4. Withdraws from pain
5. Localises pain
6. Obeys commands

Voice

1. No response
2. Incomprehensible sounds
3. Incorrect words
4. Confused
5. Normal speech

Eyes

1. No response
2. Opens eyes to pain
3. Opens eyes to speech
4. Opens eyes spontaneously

What types of intracranial bleed are you aware of, and what is the typical aetiology of each?

Intracranial bleeds can be classified as intra-axial (from within the brain itself) and extra-axial (from within the skull but outside of the brain matter).

These can be further subdivided:

Intra-axial

Intraventricular – most common in premature infants

Intracerebral – usually due to direct trauma or associated with haemorrhagic CVA

Extra-axial

Extradural – due to traumatic rupture of an artery
 – middle meningeal commonest

Subdural – due to tearing of the bridging venous sinuses
 – seen in elderly and alcoholics where cerebral atrophy places them at risk

Subarachnoid – usually from rupture of aneurysm or from arteriovenous malformation
 – can also be due to trauma

What is the Monroe-Kellie doctrine?

- This tells us that the skull encloses the brain, blood and CSF within a fixed volume, in a state of equilibrium.

- With this in mind, any increase in volume (for example from a haematoma) must be compensated for by a decrease in the volume of one of the other components.

- Initially a decrease in CSF is seen, followed by a decrease in venous flow.

- Once no more compensation is available, small increases in volume will cause massive rises in ICP.

- This principle is also used to guide treatment. For example, manipulation of cerebral blood flow can be achieved by hyperventilation and drugs (e.g. mannitol) in order to keep intracranial pressure maintained.

How is intracranial pressure (ICP) related to cerebral perfusion pressure (CPP), and give typical normal values in mmHg?

CPP = MAP − ICP

CPP = 80 − 12

CPP = 68 mm Hg

12: Portal Hypertension

What is the definition of portal hypertension?

Defined by the pressure difference between the portal system and the hepatic veins of more than 12 mmHg

What different causes of portal hypertension are you aware of?

The causes can be divided into:

Pre-hepatic

- portal vein / splenic vein thrombosis
- splenomegaly

Hepatic

- hepatitis
- cirrhosis
- schistosomiasis (commonest cause in 3rd world)

Post-hepatic

- IVC obstruction
- Budd-Chiari syndrome (obstruction of hepatic vein outflow leading to obstruction which, in Western countries, is usually by thrombosis)
- right heart failure

A patient with known portal hypertension and oesophageal varices is admitted to A&E with an upper GI bleed. Describe the principals of management ?

- ABC

- IV access and bloods for Hb, clotting and X-match are vital

- Immediate management following this should include measures to decrease portal pressure

- This can be done by:
  - Octreotide – indirectly causes splanchnic vasoconstriction thereby reducing portal pressure
  - Glypressin – causes mesenteric constriction which decreases blood flow and pressure.

- Emergency endoscopy +/- sclerotherapy or banding is now used. However, where this is not available and where other measure mentioned have failed, a Sengstaken-Blakemore tube can be placed in situ to help tamponade the bleed.

In cases where endoscopy fails (5-10%), surgical intervention is required. This can consist of a shunt procedure (Transjugular Intrahepatic Portal Systemic Shunt – TIPSS), or occasionally oesophageal transaction and devascularisation.

While TIPSS offers excellent results, it is worth remembering that, in the initial stages, encephalopathy may worsen.

Where are the sites of porto-systemic anastomosis?

There are 6 main sites of portosystemic anastomosis

Site	Systemic	Portal	Clinical Consequence
Oesophagus	Azygous vein	Left gastric vein	Oesophageal varices
Bare surface of liver	Phrenic veins	Portal veins	No clinical consequence
Umbilical region	Sub-cutaneous veins of anterior abdominal wall	Para-umbilical veins	Caput medusa
Retro-peritoneum	Veins of Posterior abdominal wall	Superior and inferior mesenteric veins	No clinical consequence
Rectum	Middle and inferior rectal veins	Superior rectal vein	Rectal varices
Patent Ductus Venosus	IVC	Portal vein	Nil

13: Fluids and Electrolytes

What is the composition of 1 litre of 0.9% normal saline, 5% dextrose, Hartmann's solution and gelofusin?

Solution	Na^+	Cl^-	K^+	Ca^{2+}	Other	pH
0.9% Normal Saline	154	154	-	-	-	5.0
5% dextrose	-	-	-	-	50g dextrose	4.0
Hartmann's Solution	131	111	5	2	29g lactate	6.5
Gelofusin	154	125	<0.4	-	40g gelatin	7.4

What is the daily requirement of a 70kg male for water, Na^+ and K^+?

Water – 35 ml/kg per day

Na^+ – 1-2 mmol/kg per day

K^+ – 1 mmol/kg per day

What are the advantages / disadvantages of colloids?

Advantages

- Have a larger molecular weight (usually >30,000) and therefore stay intravascularly for longer

- Exert oncotic pressure thereby drawing surrounding water into vascular compartment

- Compatible with other IV infusions (except those with Ca^{2+})

Disadvantages

- Expensive

- Allergenic – may cause anaphylactic reaction

- Can worsen coagulopathy

- Contain animal gelatin – unpopular with some religious groups

- Contains high amounts of chloride, with risk of hyperchloraemic acidosis if given in large quantities

14: Acute Respiratory Distress Syndrome

What do you understand by the term ARDS?

Defined by:

- Refractory hypoxia
- Acute bilateral pulmonary infiltrates
- Pulmonary artery wedge pressure (PAWP) of <18
- PaO^2 (mmHg) / FiO^2 of <200 for ARDS and < 300 for ALI (acute lung injury)

In other words, it is pulmonary oedema of non-cardiogenic source and without fluid overload.

What causes of ARDS are you aware of?

- Sepsis
- Burns
- Massive blood transfusion
- Trauma
- Pancreatitis
- Aspiration

What is the treatment?

- Treatment is mostly supportive, involving appropriate management of the underlying disease

- Patient will almost invariably require mechanical ventilation

- If mechanical ventilation alone is still not adequate, high PEEP (positive end expiratory pressure) of 10-15cm H_2O may be instituted with low tidal volumes

- Inspiratory:expiratory ratios of 1:1 may help, or even inversed ratios (increased inspiratory with decreased expiratory to allow pulmonary units to exchange more gas)

- Other measures such as prone positioning, inhaled nitric oxide or inhaled surfactant are used but have no proven mortality benefit

- The use of Extracorporeal Membrane Oxygention (ECMO) is of unknown benefit and is awaiting results from trials such as the CESAR trial

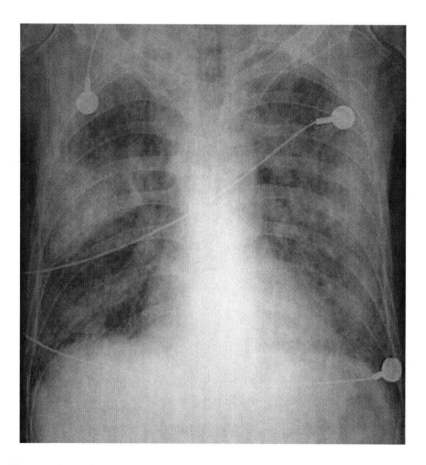

Figure 24: Chest radiograph with diffuse bilateral pulmonary infiltrates. An endotracheal tube can also be seen.

15: Shock

What is the definition of shock?

Generally, there are two main points needed to define shock.

These are:
1. Insufficient tissue perfusion
2. Leading to cellular hypoxia

What are the main types of shock?

- **Hypovolaemic** – absolute decrease in circulating volume.

- **Distributive** – where there is abnormal alteration in the body's distribution of fluid. This incorporates septic, neurogenic and anaphylactic shock.

- **Cardiogenic** – primary cardiac cause (such as post-MI).

- **Obstructive** – cardiac function is impeded indirectly (e.g. massive PE causing RV obstruction).

Can you further classify hypovolaemic shock? Which parameters alter with different grades?

	Blood loss (volume)	Blood loss (%)	BP	Pulse	U/O mls/hr	Clinically
Grade I	> 750ml	≥ 15	↔	↑ or ↔	30 +	Often normal
Grade II	< 1.5l	15-30	↓ pulse pressure	↑	20-30	Anxious
Grade III	< 2l	30-40	↓↓	↑↑	> 20	Agitated
Grade IV	< 2.5l	40 +	↓↓↓	↑↑	0	Comatose

16: Pancreatitis

What is the underlying pathological process?

Acute inflammation of the pancreas, caused by autodigestion by pancreatic enzymes.

Give a list of common causes of pancreatitis?

- Alcohol
- Gallstones
- Trauma
- Iatrogenic (ERCP, drugs such as steroids)
- Idiopathic

What scoring systems are in use?
Briefly describe one of them?

The main biological scoring systems are Glasgow and Ranson's. The Glasgow score is detailed here as it is much simpler. Ranson's scoring involves two-stage criteria, performed on admission and then reviewed again 48 hours after admission.

Glasgow Score (1 score for each positive criteria)
- Age > 55 years
- PaO^2 < 8.0 kPa (FiO_2 of 0.21)
- WCC > 15 $\times 10^9$/l
- Albumin < 32 g/L
- $Ca2^+$ < 2.00 mmol/l
- LDH > 600 U/l
- Urea > 16 mmol/l
- Blood sugar > 10 mmol/l

Glasgow Score for pancreatitis (continued)

A score of three or more suggests severe pancreatitis, and early intensive care advice should be sought.

Recent changes have removed elevation in the transaminase levels as part of scoring criteria, although many units still use them.

A CRP of >150 after 24 hours is also associated with worse outcome. Interestingly, the numerical rise in serum amylase / lipase level does not seem have any bearing on the extent or severity of pancreatitis.

Balthazar radiological scoring system

The Balthazar radiological scoring system, based on CT results, is also used to score the severity of pancreatitis:

Grade A – normal pancreas

Grade B – enlarged gland

Grade C – abnormal gland, haziness on CT

Grade D – collection / phlegmon

Grade E – two or more collections, or gas in / around pancreas

Part 3

Physiology

1: Fluid Compartments

What proportion of the body is composed of water?

About 60% of total body weight is water. This equates to approximately 42 litres in a 70 kilogram man.

How is this total body water divided between the various fluid compartments?

Total body water (TBW) is divided into two main compartments:

- Intracellular fluid – approximately 28 litres in a 70 kg man

- Extracellular fluid – approximately 14 litres in a 70 kg man
    Further divided into:
    - o Interstitial fluid – approximately 11 litres
    - o Plasma – approximately 3 litres
    - o Transcellular fluid – approximately 1 litre

What is the daily requirement of Na^+ and K^+ in an average 70 kilogram man?

The daily requirement of these solutes is dependant on a number of factors.

However, in a healthy individual, the sodium requirement can be calculated as:

- Sodium: 1.0 – 2.0 mmol/kg/day
- Potassium: 0.5 – 1.0 mmol/kg/day

2: Acids and Bases

What is the difference between an acid and a base?

An **acid** is a molecule in solution that *releases* hydrogen ions.

A **base** is a molecule in solution that *accepts* hydrogen ions.

What does the term acidity mean and how does this relate to pH?

Acidity refers to the amount of free hydrogen ions in solution. If the hydrogen ion concentration is high, then the acidity is high.

Hydrogen ion concentration is often referred to in terms of pH.

pH can be defined as: **pH = -log $\{H^+\}$**

As it is an inverse relationship, when the acidity increases, the pH decreases.

The pH of water is 7.0. This means that the hydrogen ion concentration of water is 10^{-7}.

Acid solutions have a greater concentration of hydrogen ions than water, and basic solutions have a lower concentration of hydrogen ions than water.

3: Action Potentials

What is the resting membrane potential?

This is the potential difference (i.e. charge) between the outside of a cell and the inside of a cell. The resting potential is created by the presence of excess negative ions on the inside of the cell membrane.

What factors influence the resting membrane potential?

Two main factors influence resting membrane potential:
- The difference in membrane permeability to specific ions
- The difference in the concentration of ions on either side of the membrane

These factors are influenced by the presence of specific ion transport mechanisms in the cell membrane, which pump ions into and out of the cell, thus generating the differences.

What happens in the resting state in a neurone?

In the resting state, there is an excess of potassium ions inside the cell compared to the outside of the cell. Sodium is the opposite, with low intracellular concentrations.

The key difference is that the cell membrane at rest is far more permeable to potassium ions than to sodium ions. The potassium therefore moves along a gradient out of the cell. This lead to a loss of +ve charge from the cell and a residual –ve charge within the cell. The concentration of the sodium and potassium ions is maintained by a Na^+ - K^- ATPase pump.

The resting potential in a neurone is approximately -70mV.

Draw a diagram representing an action potential and explain what is happening to cause this phenomenon?

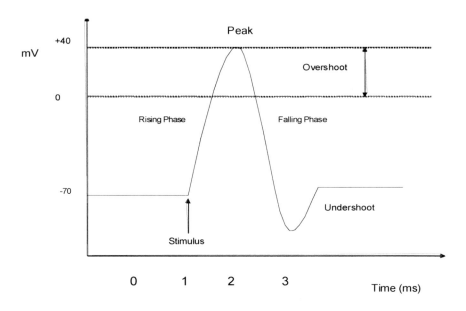

Figure 25: The action potential

An action potential (AP) is a rapid change in the membrane potential of a cell. However, not all cells are capable of creating an AP. It is most commonly associated with neurones and myocytes.

During the AP, the permeability of the cell membrane to sodium and potassium ions alters. The main change is the massive increase in permeability to sodium channels. This leads to an influx of sodium ions which in turn increases the positive charge within the cell.

What causes the potential to return to the resting voltage?

The sodium channels that open in the initiation of the AP close virtually instantaneously. This means that the rapid influx of sodium ceases.

At the same time, there is an increase in the permeability of the cell membrane to potassium. This efflux leads to a further loss of +ve ions from the cell.

What is the refractory period?

The refractory period is caused by the hyperpolarisation of the cell membrane after the AP. As a result, the cell membrane potential is more negative than the resting potential. This, in turn, prevents a further AP from being fired.

The refractory period is divided into an absolute period and a relative period.

- In the *absolute period*, an AP cannot be produced.
- In the *relative period*, an AP can be produced but only in response to a very strong stimulus.

4: Potassium Imbalance

Why is potassium an important ion?

Potassium is the most prominent intracellular ion. The extracellular concentration is far lower, and only 2% of total body potassium is found in this space.

Potassium is vital in the maintenance of the resting potential of cells. This is obviously most important in excitable tissues such as cardiac and skeletal muscles.

What are the causes of hyperkalaemia?

Failure of excretion
- Renal failure
- Drugs
    - Potassium-sparing diuretics
    - NSAIDs
    - ACE inhibitors
- Mineralocorticoid deficiency or resistance
    - Addison's disease
    - Hypoaldosteronism
    - Renal tubular acidosis
- Gordon's syndrome (a rare familial renal tubular defect)

Release from cells
- Rhabdomyolysis
- Burns
- Tumour lysis syndrome
- Massive transfusion
- Shift from cells, as seen in metabolic acidosis

Excessive intake
- Usually iatrogenic

What are the effects of hyperkalaemia?

Symptoms of hyperkalaemia tend to be quite non-specific.

They include:
- Malaise
- Palpitations
- Muscle weakness
- Symptoms of metabolic acidosis, e.g. dyspnoea
- Cardiac arrhythmia
- Sudden death

What ECG changes occur in hyperkalaemia?

An urgent ECG should be obtained in anyone thought to be hyperkalaemic or hypokalaemia.

Without treatment, dysrhythmias (VF and VT) will occur.

The characteristic ECG changes in hyperkalaemia include:
- Small P waves and increased PR interval
- Widened QRS complex
- ST depression
- Tall tented T waves
- Shortened QT interval

What are the causes of hypokalaemia?

- Insufficient intake
- Increased losses
  - o Diarrhoea
  - o Vomiting
- Drugs (very common)
  - o Diuretics (thiazide and loop diuretics)
  - o Antifungals (amphotericin)
  - o Salbutamol
- Hypomagnesaemia
- Hyperaldosteronism
  - o Renal artery stenosis
  - o Conn's syndrome
  - o Cushing's syndrome
- Over-consumption of liquorice

What are the effects of hypokalaemia?

There are frequently no symptoms at all but effects may include:
- Muscle weakness and myalgia
- Confusion and seizures
- Cardiac arrhythmias

What are the ECG changes associated with hypokalaemia?

- Flattened T waves
- ST depression
- Prolonged QT interval
- U waves

It is worth bearing in mind that there is a stronger correlation of ECG changes with hyperkalaemia than with hypokalaemia.

5: Sodium imbalance

Why is sodium an important ion?

Sodium is the most prominent extracellular ion, and is responsible for the maintenance of many cellular functions. Possibly the most important of these functions is the depolarisation of excitable cells. Sodium also plays a vital role in the maintenance of water balance in the body.

What are the causes of hypernatraemia?

- Inadequate intake of water (dehydration)
- Water loss
    o Diabetes insipidus
    o Diuretics
    o Lithium
- Conn's Syndrome
- Cushing's Syndrome
- Rarely due to ingestion of hypertonic fluids

What are the symptoms of hypernatraemia?

Symptoms are often rather subtle but can include the following:
- Lethargy
- Malaise
- Peripheral oedema
- Weakness
- Coma
- Seizures

What are the causes of hyponatraemia?

When considering the causes of hyponatraemia, it is vital to take into account the volaemic status of the patient. Almost all cases of hyponatraemia are associated with a raised serum ADH level.

- **Hypovolaemic** (ADH secretion is appropriate)

  Causes include:
  - Haemorrhage
  - Diarrhoea
  - Vomiting
  - Fistulae
  - Burns
  - Addison's disease
  - Renal failure

- **Normovolaemic** (ADH is inappropriate - i.e. SIADH)

  Causes:
  - Drugs
  - Neoplasia (especially small cell carcinoma)
  - Lung disease
    - Pneumonia
    - Abscess
  - Brain disease

- **Hypervolaemic** (this is the most common group)

  ADH is increased due to decreased circulating blood volume, although total body water is raised

  Causes include:
  - Congestive cardiac disease
  - Cirrhosis
  - Nephrotic syndrome
  - Renal failure

What are the symptoms of hyponatraemia?

Many patients with hyponatraemia are asymptomatic.

However symptoms can include:
- Nausea
- Vomiting
- Headache
- Malaise
- Coma
- Seizures

What is pseudo-hyponatraemia?

- This phenomenon is seen when plasma lipid, protein or glucose levels are raised

- It causes a shift in water from the extracellular space into the intracellular space

- This causes a falsely depressed serum sodium level

- The plasma osmolality is usually high or normal.

6: Hypercalcaemia

What are the presenting features of hypercalcaemia?

Symptoms include:

- Depression
- Malaise
- Confusion
- Anorexia
- Polyuria
- Nausea
- Vomiting
- Constipation
- Polydipsia
- Coma
- Cardiac arrhythmia (with short QT interval)
- Abdominal pains (pancreatitis, renal stones, constipation)

What are the causes of hypercalcaemia?

The two most common causes are *malignancy* and *hyperparathyroidism*. These account for over 90% of cases.

A good mnemonic to recall the more obscure causes is **chimpanzees**:

- **C**: Calcium infusion
- **H**: Hyperparathyroidism
- **I**: Idiopathic, iatrogenic
- **M**: MEN, Milk-Alkali Syndrome
- **P**: Paget's Disease
- **A**: Acromegaly
- **N**: Neoplasia
- **Z**: Zollinger-Ellison Disease
- **E**: Excess Vitamin A
- **E**: Excess Vitamin D
- **S**: Sarcoid

7: Nutrition

What are the daily nutritional requirements of patients?

There are six groups of nutrients that the body requires to sustain life.

These include:

- Carbohydrates

- Proteins

- Fats

- Vitamins

- Minerals

- Water

What is Basal Metabolic Rate (BMR), and how is it calculated?

BMR (Basal Metabolic Rate) is:

- the amount of energy expended by the body
- at rest
- at a neutral temperature
- with the digestive system inactive.

It is calculated according to the Harris-Benedict Equations which take into account sex, age, height and weight.

What factors affect Basal Metabolic Rate (BMR)?

Basal Metabolic Rate (BMR) is affected by several factors including:

- Sex
- Age
- Lean body mass
- Cardiovascular activity / fitness
- Hormonal influences
- Illness

What is the Respiratory Quotient?

The respiratory quotient represents the ratio of CO_2 produced to O_2 consumed when burning a fuel.

It is represented by the following equation:

RQ = CO_2 produced / O_2 consumed

In normal circumstances, the RQ is maximally 1.0 (although it can exceed 1.0 with certain fuels). This represents the oxidization of pure carbohydrate.

A RQ below 1.0 represents suboptimal oxidation as demonstrated by protein (0.8) and fat (0.7).

8: Pancreas

What is the function of the pancreas?

- The pancreas is an organ of both the digestive and the endocrine systems.
- It acts as both an endocrine and as an exocrine gland.

What is insulin?

- Insulin is a polypeptide hormone that is secreted from the Islets of Langerhans in the pancreas
- It has a primary role in the maintenance of carbohydrate homeostasis
- It also has an effect on the metabolism of fat and protein in the body

What other hormones are produced by the pancreas and what are their actions?

Endocrine
- Glucagon – raises blood sugar
- Somatostatin – inhibits pancreatic endocrine function
- Pancreatic polypeptide – inhibits pancreatic exocrine function

Exocrine
- Pancreatic enzymes – digestion
  - ° Amylase
  - ° Trypsin, chymotrypsin and carboxypeptidase
  - ° Lipase
- Bicarbonate ions – helps digestion by neutralizing acidic duodenal contents

What is the volume of pancreatic juice produced everyday?

Approximately 1.5 litres of pancreatic juice is produced daily in a normal feeding adult.

This amount will reduce, due to lack of stimulation, if a person does not ingest food orally.

Certain drugs, such as octreotide, will also help decrease pancreatic function and output.

How is the production of pancreatic juice regulated?

Pancreatic secretion is under both neuronal control and hormonal control.

Neuronal

- When one first thinks about or smells food, gastrin (from the antrum) is released
- This is the first step towards increased pancreatic secretion
- Following ingestion of food, gastric distension further stimulates gastrin release
- The effect of gastrin is to stimulate the vagus nerve to increase pancreatic activity (rest and digest)

Hormonal

- The duodenum, in response to food, secretes CCK and secretin
- These in turn stimulate production of enzymes as well as HCO_3^-

9: Haemostasis

What are the components involved in haemostasis?

Haemostasis refers to the physiological process whereby bleeding is stopped.

There are a number of components involved in this process:

- **Vasoconstriction** – locally to reduce blood loss

- **Primary haemostasis** – platelets adhere to the exposed collagen on the damaged vessel wall

- **Secondary haemostasis** – coagulation cascade acts to create fibrin clot

- **Fibrinolysis** – organized repair of damaged wall and break down of fibrin clot

10: Cardiac Physiology

What does the Starling Curve represent?

The Starling Curve illustrates the relationship between preload of the heart and cardiac contractility. It shows that increasing the preload (and therefore the cardiac muscle length) will lead to an increase in the contractile force of the cardiac fibres. This occurs until the myocytes are overstretched, at which point contractility decreases. This is seen clinically in cases of congestive cardiac failure.

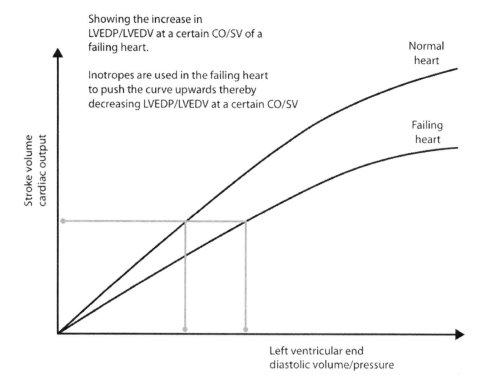

Figure 25: The Frank-Starling curve

Define cardiac output (CO)?

Cardiac output (CO) is the volume of blood being pumped by a ventricle in one minute.

Cardiac output is represented by the following equation:

CO = Stroke Volume (SV) X Heart Rate (HR)

Where:

SV = End Diastolic Volume – End Systolic Volume

Typical values are:

CO = 70mls x 70 bpm
CO = 4900 mls/min

What factors affect cardiac output?

Cardiac output (CO) is variable in any given individual.

The factors that influence Cardiac Output can be attributed to Stroke Volume (SV) and Heart Rate (HR):

- Level of physical exercise
- Sympathetic stimulation increases CO
- Parasympathetic stimulation decreases CO
- Drugs that alter the HR or cardiac contractility (inotropes/ chronotropes)

How can one measure the cardiac output?

There are a number of methods to measure the CO. These include:

The Fick Principle

This involves measuring:

- VO_2 consumption using spirometry
- Comparing the O_2 concentration in the pulmonary artery (i.e. venous blood) to the concentration in the radial artery (i.e. arterial blood)

The CO can then be calculated using the following equation:

$$CO = VO_2 / (C_{arterial} - C_{venous})$$

Cardiac Doppler Assessment

This involves the recording of Doppler frequencies on Echocardiogram. It is a simple and non-invasive method.

Pulmonary Artery Thermodilution

This involves using a Swann-Ganz Catheter to instigate a small change in the blood temperature. This thermodilution can be analysed to calculate the CO.

The same principle may be applied using chemical dilution of small quantities of drugs (for example, lithium).

11: Blood Pressure

What is blood pressure (BP)?

Blood pressure is the pressure exerted by the blood at right angles to the walls of the blood vessels. It is usually assumed that, by referring to blood pressure, one is meaning the systemic arterial pressure.

What factors affect blood pressure?

There are several factors that affect blood pressure including:

Volume of circulating blood

Circulating blood volume, which can be raised or lowered, is controlled by a number of hormonal, neuronal and extrinsic factors including:
- Renin angiotensin system (RAS)
- Aldosterone release
- ADH
- Sympathetic and parasympathetic nervous system activation
- Drugs

Peripheral vascular resistance

Once again, this can be raised or lowered according to the following factors:
- Renin angiotensin system (RAS)
- Autonomic system activation
- Drugs

Blood viscosity

This can be influenced by certain physical conditions or drugs.

How is blood pressure controlled?

The endogenous control of blood pressure is known to be influenced by the following factors:

- *Local baroreceptor reflex*: This involves the peripheral baroreceptors noting an alteration in BP. This leads to a local release of vasoactive mediators, which alter the caliber of the vascular wall. This, in turn, leads to alteration of resistance and therefore alteration of BP.

- *Renin Angiotensin System (RAS)*: This system involves detection of alteration to the arterial pressure at the juxtoglomerular apparatus. This leads to release of renin, ultimately causing angiotensin II secretion. Angiotensin II is the body's most powerful endogenous vasoconstrictor.

- *Aldosterone*: Aldosterone is released from the zona glomerusola of the adrenal cortex in response to raised angiotensin II. It stimulates retention of sodium and excretion of potassium in the renal tubules. This has the effect of increasing water retention, thereby increasing circulating blood volume.

What is autoregulation, and why is it important?

Autoregulation refers to the ability to regulate the blood pressure of a specific organ. It is a phenomenon that is unique to specific organs including the brain, the kidneys and the heart.

An important factor to be considered in autoregulation is the ability to regulate the flow of blood in the absence of autonomic control (i.e. control at a local level).

What is autoregulation (continued)

Autoregulation is important as it ensures that vital organs, such as the kidneys, are able to maintain a constant perfusion pressure. This prevents damage to the organ by perfusion pressures that are too low or too high.

Obviously, autoregulation can only ensure a homeostatic pressure when the mean arterial pressure (MAP) falls between two values. When the MAP is at extremes, then regulatory capacity is lost, and loss of control follows swiftly. This is represented in the diagram below:

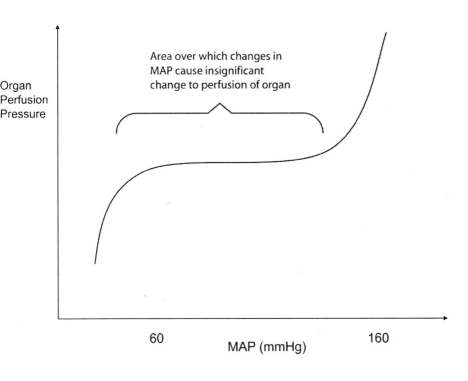

Figure 26: Autoregulation Curve

12: Gastric Physiology

What are the three phases of digestion?

Cephalic Phase

This occurs before the food enters the stomach. It involves activation of the vagus nerve as a result of experience, sight, smell and taste of food.

Gastric Phase

This phase is stimulated by distention of the stomach with food, and raised gastric pH. This leads to release of ACh, gastrin and histamine which, in turn, leads to the release of HCl.

Intestinal Phase

There are two elements to this phase:

- *Excitatory* – food enters the duodenum, and leads to duodenal gastrin and pancreatic enzymes being released.
- *Inhibitory* – alteration of duodenal pH leads to inhibition of the gastric outlet and gastric secretion.

What substances are produced by the stomach?

- Mucus – secreted by goblet cells
- Gastric acid – secreted by parietal cells
- Intrinsic factor – secreted by parietal cells
- Pepsinogen – secreted by chief cells
- Renin – secreted by chief cells
- Gastrin – secreted by G cells

How is acid produced in the stomach?

This is illustrated in the diagram below:

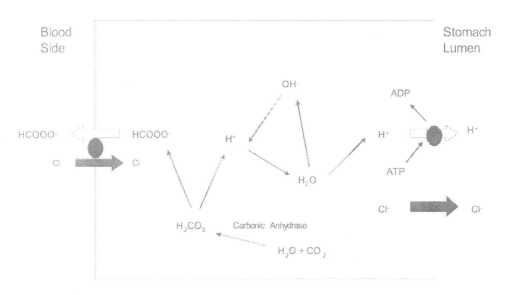

Figure 27: Gastric acid production

13: Adrenal Gland

What hormones are secreted by the adrenal gland?

Different hormones are secreted from different anatomical regions within the gland:

Adrenal cortex
- Cortisol (from zona fasciculate)
- Aldosterone (from zona glomerulosa)
- Testosterone (from zona reticularis)
- Dehydroepiandrosterone / DHEA (from zona reticularis)

Adrenal medulla
- Adrenaline
- Noradrenaline

What effect does adrenaline have on the body?

Adrenaline (epinephrine) is a cathecholamine that is synthesized from phenylalanine and tyrosine.

Adrenaline plays a key role in the body's stress response.

The physiological effects of adrenaline include:
- Increases heart rate and stroke volume
- Pupillary dilation
- Vasoconstriction of skin arterioles
- Vasodilatation of muscle arterioles
- Elevation of blood sugar

What effect does cortisol have on the body?

Cortisol has a number of effects:

- Organic metabolism
    - Stimulates protein catabolism
    - Stimulates gluconeogenesis
    - Decreases glucose tolerance
    - Breakdown of fatty acids

- Enhances vascular sensitivity to vasoconstrictors

- Inhibition of specific inflammatory responses and inflammation

14: Renal Physiology

What do you understand by the term renal clearance?

Renal clearance can be defined as:

The volume of plasma completely cleared of a specific compound per unit time and measured as a test of kidney function.

Clearance can be measured by the following equation:

$$C = (U \times F) / P$$

C = Clearance (ml/minute)

U = Urine concentration (mmol/litre)

F = Urine flow (ml/minute)

P = Plasma concentration (mmol/litre)

How is Glomerular Filtration Rate (GFR) related to clearance?

Clearance can be used to estimate glomerular filtration rate (GFR).

If a substance is completely filtered, and neither secreted nor reabsorbed, it can be used to calculate the GFR.

The best substance for measuring GFR is Insulin. However this is rarely used in practice.

A commonly used parameter is creatinine clearance. Creatinine is only minimally secreted in the renal tubules, and therefore provides a good estimate of the GFR.

What are normal Glomerular Filtration Rate values?

The normal value for GFR is:

Males: 97 – 137 ml/min
Females: 88 – 128 ml/min

Note GFR decreases with age.

Why do diabetic patients have glycosuria when glucose is reabsorbed by the kidney?

Renal plasma threshold is the concentration at which the kidney is no longer able to prevent excretion of a substance. The renal plasma threshold for glucose is 180-200 mg per 100ml. When the filtered glucose level is higher than this, the renal tubule transport mechanisms act to reabsorb glucose. In diabetes, the plasma glucose levels are very high, and these reabsorption mechanisms are saturated, leading to glucose excretion.

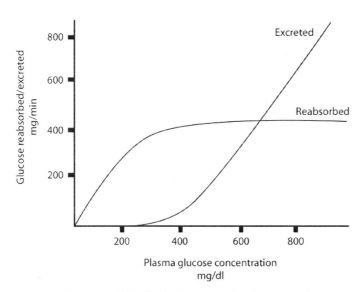

Figure 28: Relationship between plasma
Glucose load and reabsorbtion

15: Metabolic Disturbances

What are the causes of metabolic acidosis?

The causes of metabolic acidosis are best considered according to their anion gap. The anion gap is the difference between the negatively and positively charged ions in the plasma:

$$\text{Anion gap} = \{Na^+ + K^+\} - \{Cl^- + HCO_3^-\}$$

Normal range is 4-12 mmol/litre

Increased Anion Gap

Remember the mnemonic **MUDPILES**:

M - Methanol

U - Uraemia

D - Diabetic ketoacidosis

P - Paraldehyde

I - Infection

L - Lactic acidosis

E - Ethanol

S - Salicylates

No Increase in Anion Gap

- Diarrhoea
- Fistulae
- Renal failure
- Drugs (especially acetazolamide)

What are the blood gas findings in metabolic acidosis?

The key findings are:

- Low pH
- Low bicarbonate
- Negative base excess
- Often decreased CO_2 due to Kussmaul's respiration

What are the causes of metabolic alkalosis?

When considering the causes of metabolic alkalosis, classify as:

- Loss of H^+ - usually due to vomiting
- Shift of H^+ into the intracellular space - usually due to hypokalaemia
- Bicarbonate infusion

What are the causes of respiratory alkalosis?

This phenomenon is due to hyperventilation, caused by:

- Anxiety
- Pain
- Altitude
- Pyrexia which stimulates the ventilatory center
- Pregnancy
- CNS causes (CVA, meningitis)

What are the causes of respiratory acidosis?

These can be acute or chronic:

Acute

Essentially failure of ventilation:
- Head injury with respiratory centre depression
- Neuromuscular failure (Guillian-Barre syndrome, myasthenia gravis)
- Airway obstruction

Chronic
- COPD (most common)
- Obesity hypoventilation syndrome
- Amyotrophic lateral sclerosis

16: Respiration

Draw a diagram representing a spirometry trace, and label each part?

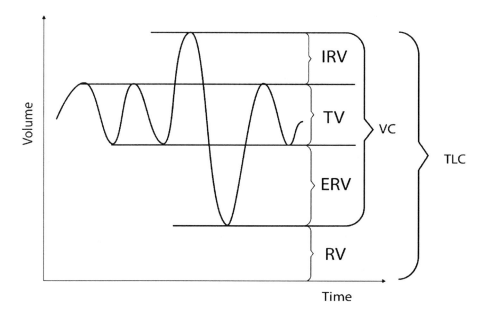

Figure 29: Lung volumes and capacities

- IRV (Inspiratory Reserve Volume) = 3.0 litres
- TV (Tidal Volume) = 500-700 ml
- ERV (Expiratory Reserve Volume) = 2.0 litres
- RV (Residual Volume) = 2 litres
- VC (Vital Capacity) = 5.5 litres
- TLC (Total Lung Capacity) = 7.5 litres

Values are approximate, and will vary with age, size and gender

What is dead space?

Dead space refers to the volume of air that is inhaled but takes no part in gaseous exchange.

It can be subdivided into:

- *Anatomical dead space* – this refers to the gas which is not in the alveoli. In other words the gas in the mouth, trachea, and bronchi. It is usually about 150 ml.

- *Alveolar dead space* – this is the area in the alveoli where gaseous exchange does not occur. This air does reach the alveoli but, as there is no blood supply to allow exchange, it becomes a mismatch. It is very small in healthy lungs but is of great importance in lung disease.

The sum of these is known as the physiological dead space

What is pulmonary shunt?

Pulmonary shunt occurs when there is perfusion of the alveoli, but ventilation fails to supply the perfused area.

Why is the O_2 curve sigmoid in shape?

Haemoglobin has the ability to bind four oxygen molecules. The sigmoid shape of the curve is due to the chemical interactions between the oxygen molecules and haemoglobin.

The first oxygen molecule binds to haemoglobin with difficulty. Once bound, this improves the affinity of the haemoglobin for oxygen molecules. The subsequent two molecules bind easily but the fourth oxygen molecule binds with difficulty once more.

What causes the O_2 curve to shift right and left?

The following cause left shift (i.e. increased affinity for oxygen):

- Low temperature

- Low DPG

- Low pCO_2

- Alkalosis

The following cause a right shift (i.e. decreased affinity for oxygen):

- High temperature

- High DPG

- High pCO_2

- Acidosis

Part 4

Pathology

1: Clostridia

What type of bacteria are clostridia?

Clostridia are gram positive spore-producing bacteria that grow in anaerobic conditions.

What species of clostridium are you aware of, and what diseases are associated with them?

Clostridium Perfringens (formally Welchii) – commonly associated with gas gangrene, which is an acute surgical emergency. This condition is frequently associated with contamination of surgical and traumatic wounds. Incidentally, it has also been linked with illegal abortion.

Clostridium Difficile – associated with pseudomembranous colitis. This condition manifests by the overgrowth of C. Difficile in preference for other intestinal commensal organisms. It is usually associated with the use of broad spectrum antibiotics. Pseudomembranous colitis may occur without C. Difficile being present.

Clostridium Botulinum – this bacterium typically proliferates in poorly sterilised canned foods. The bacterium releases a neurotoxin that blocks the release of acetyl-choline (ACh) at the neuromuscular junction. This in turn leads to onset of paralysis of skeletal muscles and respiratory arrest.

Clostridium Tetani – associated with tetanus. This condition is usually a result of heavy contamination of wounds. The bacterium produces a neurotoxin (tetanospasmin) which stimulates the neuromuscular junction.

Briefly describe how you would treat each species of clostridium?

Clostridium Perfringens

- Essential to diagnose early
- ABC
- Patient requires urgent widespread debridement
- Often require HDU or ITU support
- High dose intravenous antibiotics
- Second look to debride further tissue if necessary
- Use of hyperbaric O_2 advocated by some

Clostridium Difficile

- Diagnosis based on clinical suspicion and positive stool toxins
- Isolate patient and barrier nurse
- Stop any causative antibiotics
- Treatment is usually oral metronidazole or vancomycin
- Need to address often significant fluid and electrolyte imbalances
- Regular abdominal examination and X-rays as toxic megacolon is a not uncommon consequence
- If sepsis worsening, or megacolon, consider surgical intervention
- Total colectomy

Clostridium Botulinum

- Once again focus should be on prevention (i.e. good food production standards)
- Treatment of the infection includes antibiotics and supportive measures (including ventilation)

Clostridium Tetani

- Focus should be on prevention (i.e. vaccination of all children)
- Dirty wounds should be cleaned immediately, with debridement if required
- If patient is not vaccinated, or unsure of status, then vaccinate with toxoid
- If high risk wound, consider immunoglobulin
- Treatment of tetanus itself includes immunoglobulin infusion, antibiotics and supportive measures

2: Amyloid

What is amyloid?

Amyloid is a pathologic proteinaceous substance that is deposited in the extracellular space as a result of a number of clinical conditions.

It is stained with Congo Red and appears as apple green birefringence on polarised microscopy. Of interest, the human body has no enzyme capable of breaking down amyloid due to its β pleated sheet pattern.

The name amyloid comes from the Latin *amylum* meaning starch-like. This comes about from Virchow's description as it was initially found to stain similarly to starch using iodine and sulphuric acid.

What sub-types of amyloid exist?

There are 15 different sub-types of amyloid. The most interesting of these can be remembered by the mnemonic *FLASH*:

AF – pre-albumin amyloid found in familial Mediterranean fever

AL – light chain amyloid which is derived from plasma cells and seen in myeloma

AA – reactive amyloid that is produced in chronic inflammatory diseases such as rheumatoid arthritis

AS – found in Alzheimer's disease

AH – associated with haemodialysis where the protein is too small to be filtered and therefore stays in the body

What diseases can lead to amyloid deposition?

Amyloid can be sub-divided into primary and secondary:

Primary amyloid

Associated with immunocyte dyscrasias (e.g. multiple myeloma)

Secondary amyloid

Any disease that can cause chronic inflammation can lead to amyloid formation. Good examples include:

- **Infection** – e.g. tuberculosis
- **Autoimmune disease** – e.g. rheumatoid arthritis, ankylosing spondylitis, inflammatory bowel disease
- **Heroin users** – subcutaneous injections
- **Ageing**
- **Endocrine** – diabetes mellitus, thyroiditis
- **Neoplasms** – especially Hodgkin's disease and renal cell carcinoma

What organs may be affected by amyloid?

Any organ can be affected by amyloid deposition.

Organs commonly affected include:
- Kidneys
- Adrenal glands
- Liver
- Spleen
- Lung
- Thyroid
- Lymphatic tissue
- Heart
- GI Tract

3: Tumour Staging and Grading

What is the difference between staging and grading?

Staging is a method of assessing the extent of a tumour. It considers the size of the primary tumour, the presence of affected lymphatic tissue and the presence of blood borne metastasis.

Grading is a method for assessing the cancer cells in terms of their degree of differentiation and the number of mitosis. It is generally considered that high grade tumours are poorly differentiated, and correlate with increased tumour aggressiveness.

Generally, staging is of greater prognostic value than grading. The main exception to this being sarcoma.

What staging systems do you know of for colorectal carcinoma?

The most important staging system in use for colorectal carcinoma is the Dukes Staging System.

A - Tumour confined to the mucosa

B1 - Tumour invading into the muscularis mucosa

B2 - Tumour invading through the muscularis mucosa

C1 - Lymph node involvement (not apical)

C2 - Apical lymph node affected

D - With distant metastasis

This classification was described by Cuthbert Duke Esquire in 1932, and was initially for rectal carcinoma only. Since then, numerous modifications have been made to his original classification, but the essence remains the same. The TNM classification is also commonly used.

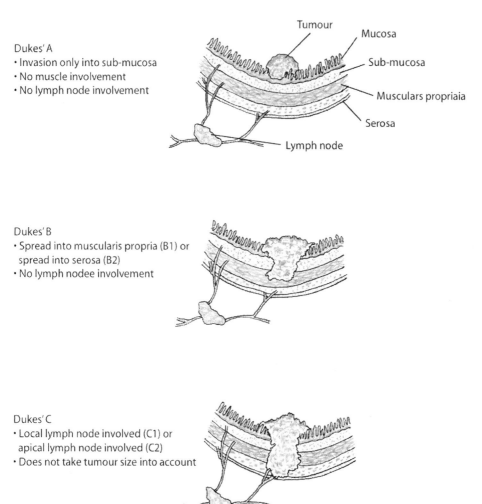

Dukes' A
· Invasion only into sub-mucosa
· No muscle involvement
· No lymph node involvement

Tumour
Mucosa
Sub-mucosa
Musculars propriaia
Serosa
Lymph node

Dukes' B
· Spread into muscularis propria (B1) or spread into serosa (B2)
· No lymph nodee involvement

Dukes' C
· Local lymph node involved (C1) or apical lymph node involved (C2)
· Does not take tumour size into account

Figure 30: The Dukes' staging for colonic carcinoma

What is the mortality associated with Dukes' classification?

A - 90% five year survival

B - 70% five year survival

C - 30% five year survival

D - 5% five year survival

4: Inflammation

What are the cardinal features of acute inflammation?

The first four cardinal features have been known since ancient times, when Celsius described them. The last feature was later described by Galen:

1. Rubor (red)

2. Calor (heat)

3. Tumor (swelling)

4. Dolor (pain)

5. Functio Laesa (loss of function)

What cell types are involved in acute inflammation?

The extravasation of leucocytes into damaged tissue is a vital part of the acute inflammatory process. These cells have a role in phagocytosis, as well as the release of several inflammatory mediators that are responsible for the acute inflammatory response.

The type of leucocyte found in inflamed tissue varies with time following the injurious event. Neutrophils are predominant during the first 24 hours. After this time, they are replaced by monocytes. In viral infections, lymphocytes are also predominant in inflamed tissue.

What are the stages of acute inflammation?

- Changes in vessel calibre – vasoconstriction.

- Endothelial damage releases histamine and other such substances causing increased vessel permeability. This allows neutrophils to extravasate into the surrounding tissue.

- Formation of fluid and cellular exudate.

- Neutrophils move to site of injury following a chemotactic gradient.

- Activation of complement, coagulation and fibrinolysis pathways.

- Release of chemical mediators, which help opsonise bacteria by attaching to their cell walls.

- Phagocytosis– macrophages arrive later and, along with neutrophils, they remove debris and bacteria from the injury site.

What are the sequelae of acute inflammation?

- Resolution

- Supporation

- Organisation

- Chronic Inflammation

5: Osteomyelitis

What is osteomyelitis?

Osteomyelitis is the inflammation of bone and bone marrow. It is almost always caused by infection.

What is the commonest organism implicated in osteomyelitis?

Any organism can cause osteomyelitis, with bacterial causes being the most common by far.

The source of infection can either be direct or haematogenous.

Staph Aureus is the most common causative organism (80%).

Other organisms to consider are E Coli, Streptococci, Salmonella and Pseudomonas. Haemophilus is rare cause owing to the vaccination

It is worth noting that, in approximately 50% of cases, no organism can be isolated.

What are the stages of acute osteomyelitis?

- Usually starts with infection at metaphysis
- Periosteal elevation
- Pus develops
- Sequestrum
- Involucrum
- Cloaca
- Either sinus or spread of sepsis or both

What X-ray changes may be seen in acute osteomyelitis?

- X-ray changes usually develop late, classically after 10 days

- After 3 weeks, 90% of radiographs will be abnormal

- May see periosteal elevation and new bone deposition

- Surrounding tissue inflammation may be evident

What are the risk factors for osteomyelitis?

- Diabetes

- Sickle cell disease

- IV drug users

- Immunosupression (e.g. AIDS or steroid use)

- Chronic joint disease

- Open fractures

- Orthopaedic surgery

- Septicaemia (especially in children)

6: Aortic Dissection

What is an aortic dissection?

Aortic dissection is disruption of the layers of the arterial wall, leading to the passage of blood between the laminar planes of the media.

This, in turn, leads to sub-intimal haematoma formation. The damage caused, and the associated pressure effect, poses risk of rupture of the vessel and subsequent massive haemorrhage.

What age group is most affected by aortic dissection, and what are the commonest causes?

Aortic dissection tends to occur in two distinct groups:

1. *40 to 60 year olds (typically males)*: with hypertension being the most common underlying factor (~90%)

2. *Younger (<40 years old)*: these patients tend to have an underlying connective tissue disease (e.g. Marfan Syndrome)

There are a number of other causes to consider:

- Trauma, particularly deceleration injury as in road traffic collisions

- Iatrogenic causes are increasing with the increasing popularity of interventional radiology

- Increased risk in pregnant women

How are aortic dissections classified?

There are two main classification systems:

Debakey

Type I – Involving the arch of aorta and descending aorta
Type II – Involving the ascending aorta only
Type III – Involving the descending aorta only

Stanford

Type A – involves the ascending aorta
Type B – involves the descending aorta

Note that Stanford Type A is the commonest, and also has the worst prognosis.

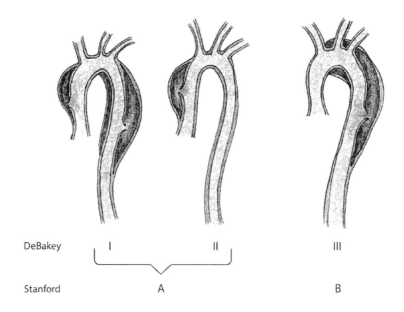

Figure 31: Classification of aortic dissection

What are the clinical features that would lead you to suspect an aortic dissection?

- Classical presentation includes sudden onset chest pain that radiates to the back
- The patient will frequently have collapsed, and may present in shock
- Peripheral pulses may be absent or asymmetrical
- ECG usually reveals ST changes that are in keeping with myocardial ischaemia and infarction
- Chest X-ray will usually reveal a widened mediastinum

Diagnosis may be confirmed by:
- CT scan
- MRI
- Transoesophageal echo
- Angiography

What is the mortality associated with aortic dissection?

As previously mentioned, Stanford Type A are the commonest aortic dissection and have the highest mortality.

Type B aortic dissections may be managed conservatively. Surgery for Type B dissections is associated with risk of postoperative paraplegia.

Overall the mortality can be estimated at 40% in early stages, and up to 80% in two weeks.

7: Skin Cancer

What features of a lesion would lead you to suspect a malignant melanoma?

Remember **ABCD**:

Asymmetry

Border – irregular

Colour – Uneven, black or red

Diameter – greater than 6mm

Other signs that suggest a sinister lesion include:
- New palpable lesion underlying
- Bleeding
- Itching
- Redness or swelling beyond the mole
- Satellite lesion

What are the main types of skin cancer?

- Malignant Melanoma
- Basal Cell Carcinoma
- Squamous Cell Carcinoma
- Merkel Cell Carcinoma (rare)

What are the staging systems for malignant melanoma, and what is the clinical relevance of staging?

The two main staging systems in use are the Breslow System and the Clark System.

Breslow System

This is the most important staging system to understand and apply.

Five year survival with Breslow thickness:
- <0.75 mm = 95-100%
- 0.76-1.49 mm = 80-95%
- 1.5-3.99 mm = 50-75%
- >4.0 mm = <50%

Clark System

Clark's staging looks at the level of invasion according to the cellular level:
- Stage I   – Invasion into epidermis only
- Stage II – Invasion into papillary dermis
- Stage III – Spans papillary dermis
- Stage IV – Invasion into reticular dermis
- Stage V – invasion of subcutaneous tissue

Clark's system, although still used, is largely thought to be not as accurate as the Breslow System. This is because the thickness of the skin layers is not uniform throughout the body

What resection margins have been suggested in the treatment of malignant melanoma?

Historically, these have been very large.

Now we tend to favour:

- Impalpable lesions – 1 cm
- Palpable – 2 cm
- Grossly nodular – 3 cm

What are the main sub-groups of multiple melanoma?

- Superficial spreading – commonest and best prognosis
- Nodular – worst prognosis as it spreads in vertical phase
- Acral lentiginous
- Lentigo maligna

8: Abscess

What is the definition of an abscess?

An abscess is a fluid-filled cavity (usually pus) that is lined by granulation tissue.

What are sterile abscesses, and how may they be caused?

A sterile abscess contains no debris or bacterial cells. It is most commonly seen where an abscess has been treated with a course of antibiotics or, more rarely, when an inappropriate intramuscular injection has been given.

What is the treatment for abscesses?

The natural history of an abscess is to drain via the path of least resistance.

Management of most abscesses will follow these steps:

- Diagnosis and recognition

- Incision and drainage

- Pus sample sent for culture and sensitivity

- Debridement of any necrotic tissue

- Leave wound open (usually with a wick or drain) to allow healing by secondary intention

- Antibiotics are considered if the patient is septic

9: Helicobacter Pylori

What are the specific features of H. Pylori?

Helicobacter Pylori are gram-negative rods that are motile (due to flagellae) and have the ability to convert urea to ammonia. This is advantageous for the organism as the chemical reaction leads to an increase in the gastric pH. As a result, it is the only known organism that is able to survive in the hostile gastric environment.

What diseases have been implicated with H. Pylori?

- Chronic gastritis
- Gastric ulcer disease
- Duodenal ulcer disease
- Gastric carcinoma / MALT
- Oesophageal carcinoma

Incidentally there are also associations with ischaemic heart disease, haematological malignancy, cot death and autoimmune disease (e.g. Sjögren's Syndrome)

What diagnostic methods are in everyday use?

- Blood antibody
- Stool antigen tests
- Carbon urea breath test
- Rapid urease test
- Histological (from biopsy)
- Microbial culture

What is the treatment of H. Pylori?

In simple cases, the standard treatment revolves around the Triple Therapy regime.

This constitutes a two-week course of:

- a Proton Pump Inhibitor (e.g. Lansoprazole 30mg BD)

and two of:

- Amoxicillin 1g BD
- Clarithromycin 500mg BD
- Metronidazole 400mg BD

A one-week regime is the first line treatment, and will eradicate the infection in approximately 85% of cases.

The two-week regime may offer higher eradication rates. However, there is a higher incidence of adverse effects, as well as poorer reported compliance.

10: Haematuria

How do you approach an elderly patient with macroscopic haematuria?

An elderly patient with macroscopic haematuria must be considered to have a malignancy until proven otherwise. The approach to this patient should be a good systematic history and examination. One should pay particular attention to recent lower urinary tract symptoms.

The investigations that should be requested are as follows:
- *Simple investigations* – urine dipstix and MC+S
- *Blood tests* – FBC, U+E, Coagulation
- *Radiology* – KUB and Ultrasound now favoured over IVU
- *Invasive investigations* – Flexible cystoscopy +/- biopsy

Essentially, one should assume that the source of bleeding could originate anywhere along the renal tract, and investigation should be systematic to reflect this.

What are the causes of haematuria?

The causes are probably best subdivided using anatomical origin (renal, ureteric, bladder, prostate and urethra) or according to a surgical sieve as below:

- Cancer
- Calculi
- Inflammatory
- Infection
- Trauma
- Iatrogenic
- Vascular (i.e. AV malformations)

What are the other specific causes of haematuria?

There are some particular causes for each anatomical site that should be recalled.

These include:

- Bladder – Schistosomiasis (common in developing world)

- Kidney – Berger's Disease (IgA nephropathy)

- Urethra – Deliberate self harm / foreign body

11: Thyroid Cancers

What types of thyroid cancer do you know of?

Carcinoma of the thyroid gland can originate from follicular cells, parafollicular cells or lymphatic tissue.

The types of thyroid cancers can be subdivided as follows:

Originating from follicular cells:

- Papillary – comprises over 80% of all thyroid cancers

- Follicular – comprises approximately 15% of all thyroid cancers

- Anaplastic – rapidly progressive with very poor prognosis. Occurs most commonly in patients over 60 years of age. Relatively rare, accounts for less than 5% of all thyroid malignancies.

Originating from parafollicular (C) Cells:

- Medullary – commonly presents as a single lump. Associated with MEN Types IIa, and IIb in about 20% of cases. Spreads to lymph nodes and occasionally haematogenously.

Originating from lymphatic tissue:

- Lymphoma – rare, less than 2% of cases. Usually Non-Hodgkin lymphoma.

What are the main features of papillary thyroid carcinoma?

Papillary carcinoma is the commonest type of thyroid cancer. It affects females three times more commonly than males. It is more common in younger patients (usually between ages 20-40).

Papillary carcinoma is characterised by presentation of a lump (multifocal in the majority of cases) in the neck. It may be associated with lymphatic spread, but the presence of lymphatic involvement is interestingly not associated with adverse outcome.

Papillary carcinoma is very strongly associated with exposure to ionizing radiation (as demonstrated by survivors of the Chernobyl disaster or atomic bombs having greatly increased incidence).

Histologically, the cells display so called 'Orphan Annie nuclei' (nuclei containing finely dispersed chromatin) and psammoma bodies (calcified structures).

What are the technical difficulties in diagnosing follicular thyroid carcinoma?

Patients will typically undergo U/S scan and FNA. Presence of follicular cells does not mean carcinoma. Patients should be counseled that this represents a 20% chance of having a malignant lesion, and that thyroidectomy should be the next step to rule it out. Frozen section, although available, is not used due to low sensitivity and the possibility of false positives.

12: Fracture Healing

What are the stages involved with long bone healing?

Inflammatory Phase (within first 3 days)

Haemorrhage and haematoma – this occurs immediately after the fracture. Role is to seal the fracture site.

Inflammation – Influx of inflammatory cells leading to break down of bone fragments.

Reparative Phase (3 days to 2 weeks)

Soft tissue callus – haematoma is organised and reabsorbed. Framework for fracture healing is laid down.

Bony callus – mineralization and strengthening of the soft tissue callus.

Remodeling Phase (lasts several years)

Ossification – occurs endochondrally to further strengthen the callus. This is reabsorbed over time, and replaced by true lamellar bone.

What factors affect fracture healing?

Patient Factors

- Age

- Co-morbid disease (e.g. diabetes mellitus)

- Smoking

- Drugs (especially steroids)

- Nutrition

Wound Factors

- Infection

- Foreign bodies (e.g. soft tissue interposition)

- Movement at fracture site (too much or too little movement having adverse effects)

13: Inflammatory Bowel Disease

What are the main differences between Crohn's disease and ulcerative colitis?

Crohn's Disease

- Mouth to anus (any segment of the gut can be affected)
- Presence of skip lesions
- Affects full thickness of mucosa
- Non-caseating granuloma formation
- Fissuring of mucosa leading to fistula formation
- Weaker association with carcinoma than ulcerative colitis
- Smoking is a risk factor for Crohn's disease

Ulcerative Colitis

- Usually commences distally and moves proximally
- Affects only large bowel (apart from backwash ileitis)
- Partial thickness mucosal involvement
- No granuloma formation
- Fistula formation is rare
- High risk of colon cancer and duodenal carcinoma
- Smoking is protective against ulcerative colitis

What are the extra-intestinal manifestations of ulcerative colitis?

- *Eyes* – uveitis, iritis, episcleritis
- *Joints* – arthritis, ankylosing spondylitis, sacroiliitis
- *Skin* – pyoderma gangrenosum, erythema nodosum
- *Liver* – primary biliary cirrhosis, hepatitis, sclerosing cholangitis
- *Cardiorespiratory* – pleural and pericardial effusions, pulmonary fibrosis

What are the indications for surgical management of ulcerative colitis?

- Failed medical management
- Perforation
- Toxic megacolon
- Cancer
- Haemorrhage

What is a granuloma?

A granuloma is a focal inflammatory process characterised by a collection of mature macrophages surrounded by a ring of lymphocytes.

14: Surgical Bacteriology

How can you classify different types of bacteria into groups, and give examples of each group?

Bacteria are prokaryocytes. They do not have a nucleus or other membrane-bound organelles.

Most bacteria are either spherical (cocci) or rod-shaped (bacilli).

Many bacteria exist as single cells. However, some bacteria characteristically clump together as diploids, chains or clusters.

The most useful way to differentiate bacteria is according to the structure of their cellular wall.

This forms the basis for Gram +ve and Gram −ve staining of bacteria. The cell wall of the Gram +ve bacteria is thick and made of many layers. The cell wall in Gram −ve bacteria is thin and has a second membranous layer. This layer is constituted of lipoproteins and lipopolysaccharides.

Other ways to distinguish bacteria involve:
- Identification of special cellular structures (e.g. flagellae)
- Identification of their action in certain environments (e.g. anaerobic versus aerobic)

How does mycobacteria gram stain?

Mycobacteria should not be classified by the Gram stain as they do not take up the crystal violet stain. They are more accurately classed as alcohol and acid fast bacilli (AAFB). They have a thick waxy outer cell wall which gives them the ability to resist most dyes. However, they can be stained using a special carbol fuchsin stain (Ziel-Neelsen stain) which produces a red discolouration.

Give examples of the main bacterial groups?

Gram +ve cocci: Staphylococcus, Streptococcus

Gram +ve bacilli: Clostridia, Actinomycoses

Gram –ve cocci: Neisrriea, Moraxella

Gram –ve bacilli: H. Pylori, Pseudomonas

Which cancer, if any, may be caused by bacteria?

The relationship between bacteria and cancer is not nearly as strong as that found with viruses. There are very few examples of the connection, and the evidence is inconclusive.

The best and most researched example is H. Pylori causing gastric carcinoma. It may also be linked with certain forms of lymphoma.

15: Surgical Virology

How can viruses be sub-divided, and give examples of each group?

Viruses can be classified in a number of different ways. A useful classification system is the Baltimore system.

This system places a virus into one of seven groups based on:
- RNA versus DNA
- Single versus double stranded
- Method of replication

This lead to the following groupings:
1. Double stranded DNA viruses (e.g. herpes, EBV, CMV)
2. Single stranded DNA viruses (e.g. parvovirus)
3. Double stranded RNA viruses (e.g. rotavirus)
4. Positive sense single stranded RNA viruses (e.g. hepatitis A, Hepatitis C, SARS)
5. Negative sense single stranded RNA viruses (e.g. ebola, influenza, measles)
6. Reverse transcribing diploid single stranded RNA viruses (e.g. HIV)
7. Reverse transcribing circular double stranded DNA viruses (e.g. hepatitis B)

Which cancers may be caused by viruses?

- Hepatocellular carcinoma – Hepatitis B and Hepatitis C
- Anal and cervical carcinoma – HPV
- Kaposi's sarcoma – HIV
- Burkett's lymphoma and nasopharyngeal carcinoma – EBV

16: Immunodeficiency

What types of immunodeficiency do you know of?

Immunodeficiency describes a state in which the immune system's capability to fight disease has been compromised or is absent.

Immunodeficiency may be divided into primary and secondary causes:

Primary

B cell deficiencies
- X-linked agammaglobulinaemia
- Selective immune deficiency

T cell deficiencies
- DiGeorge syndrome

Combined T and B cell deficiencies
- Severe Combined Immunodeficiency Disease (SCID)

Also complement deficiency and phagocyte deficiency.

Secondary

- Blood disorders – multiple myeloma
                            chronic lymphocytic leukaemia

- Chronic illness – diabetes mellitus

- Drugs – especially steroids
                disease modifying anti-rheumatic drugs

- AIDS

What types of immunoglobulin occur in the body?

There are 5 types of antibody in the body:

- IgA – found on mucosal lining
- IgD – antigen receptor on B Cells
- IgE – binds to allergens and involved in anaphylaxis
- IgG – antibody based immunity
- IgM – secreted from B cells

17: Aneurysms

What is an aneurysm?

An aneurysm is a localised abnormal dilation of a blood vessel or heart chamber.

How may aneurysms be sub-divided?

There are a number of ways to classify aneurysms:

True versus False

A true aneurysm will contain all of the layers of the vessel wall. A false aneurysm will typically involve a breach in the intimal layer of the vessel, leading to an extravacular haematoma. False aneurysms are usually associated with trauma, and true aneurysms are associated with atherosclerosis.

By Cause

- Traumatic
- Infective (e.g. mycotic)
- Inflammatory
- Congenital
- Immunological (e.g. Kawasaki's disease)

By Shape

- Fusiform – the aneurysm extends the full circumference of the vessel
- Saccular – the aneurysm only affects a proportion of the circumference of the vessel

What are the complications of aneurysms?

- Thrombosis

- Embolus

- Distal insufficiency

- Fistula formation

- Rupture

- Dissection

- Pressure on surrounding anatomical structures

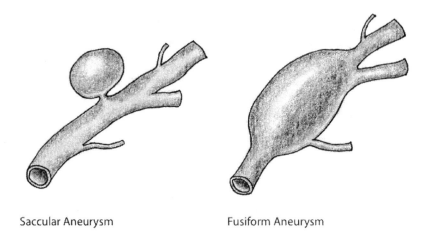

Saccular Aneurysm   Fusiform Aneurysm

Figure 32: Morphology of aneurysms

Notes

Notes

Notes

Notes

Printed in the United Kingdom
by Lightning Source UK Ltd.
136261UK00001B/195/P